A SATANIC AFFAIR

A SATANIC AFFAIR

*Salman Rushdie
and the Rage of Islam*

MALISE RUTHVEN

Chatto & Windus
LONDON

Published in 1990 by
Chatto & Windus Ltd
20 Vauxhall Bridge Road
London SW1V 2SA

A CIP catalogue record for this book is available
from the British Library.

ISBN 0 7011 3591 3

Printed and bound in Great Britain by
Mackays of Chatham, plc, Chatham, Kent.

Contents

Prologue 1

1 Satanic Fictions 11

2 Honour and Shame 29

3 Islam in Britain 54

4 Conspiracy 81

5 Ayatollahs of the North 104

6 The Word and the Text 131

Conclusion 151

Sources 165

Acknowledgements 175

Index 177

To Grey and Neiti

Prologue

27 MAY 1989

They came in their thousands from Bradford and Dewsbury, Bolton and Macclesfield, the old industrial centres; from outer suburbs like Southall and Woking; from Stepney and White-chapel in London's East End, from the cities of Wolverhampton, Birmingham, Manchester and Liverpool. They wore white hats and long baggy trousers with flapping shirt tails. Most of them were bearded; the older men looked wild and scraggy with curly, grey-flecked beards – they were mountain men from Punjab, farmers from the Ganges delta, peasants from the hills of Mirpur and Campbellpur. After decades of living in Britain, they still seemed utterly *foreign*: even in Hyde Park, a most cosmopolitan part of a very cosmopolitan city, where Arab families foregather in summer, where French, Spanish and Dutch are spoken sooner than English, they were aliens. They were not sophisticated, suave metropolitans like the blacks – the Afro-Caribbeans – with whom the racists and anti-racists banded them; they seemed like men from the sticks, irredeem-ably provincial.

The banners proclaimed, among other things, a literacy in English recently achieved: 'Freedom of speech, yes! Freedom to insult no!' 'Penguin will pay for its crims!' As well as defiance there were pleas for acceptance: 'Islam is not bigoted, intolerant or unjust: for proof read the writings of Shaw, Briffault, Lamar-tine and others'; 'Rousseau greatest champion of human liberty and equality deeply inspired by the Prophet Muhammad'; '"Islam is the only suitable creed for Europe" George Bernard Shaw'; 'Dr John W. Baker: "Islam the greatest blessing for mankind."' But there was no mistaking the central thrust of

1

the message: 'Rushdie is a devil!' 'Rushdie is a son of Satan!'
'Kill the bastard!' 'Jihad on agnostics!' 'The devil is reincarnated
in Rushdie!' 'Devil Rushdie wanted dead or alive!' Some were
even uglier: alongside a gallows with a devil-horned Rushdie
hanging in effigy there grinned the novelist's familiar, balding
features affixed to the body of a pig. Around its neck the
five-pronged Star of David testified to the view, widely-held
among Muslims, that the whole Rushdie affair was a Zionist
plot to undermine Islam. Seeing me with my notebook a man
approached and asked if I was a reporter. He was in his thirties,
handsome, moustached, with a touch of aggressiveness in his
manner.

'Actually I'm writing a book,' I said. 'Have you read *The
Satanic Verses*?'

'I've read some extracts. It's filthy language used. Lavatorial
language. There's a big conspiracy behind it. A lot of money.
The guy's certainly been bribed. Five hundred thousand now,
three hundred thousand later. Zionist conspiracy, American
conspiracy. European governments in it as well.'

'It's easy to see conspiracies where there are none.'

'You may not believe what we are saying,' said the man,
becoming more heated. 'But this book is totally filthy. He should
be making money some other way. Just withdraw the book,'
he urged, as if it were my decision. 'Problem solved.'

'There are many books in libraries which say worse things
about Islam than Rushdie does. Do you think they should be
banned as well? What about Dante? Do you know what he said
about the Prophet?'

I wouldn't have repeated it even if I had known the lines by
heart, not at that time in that place. The poet puts Muhammad
and Ali, a scarcely less revered figure in Islam, along with other
sowers of discord and schism, in the ninth *bolgia* or gulf of the
eighth circle of hell, where he suffers perpetual torment:

　　No cask stove in by cant or middle ever
　　So gaped as one I saw there, from the chin
　　Down to the fart-hole split as by a cleaver

His tripes hung by his heels; the pluck and spleen
Showed with the liver the sordid sack
That turns to dung the food it swallows in . . .[1]

'Who's Dante?' said the man. 'Listen to me. You are Christian
and you can say "I don't want to have anything to do with
Muslims." OK. We won't be upset. But don't say something
false, totally false about us. Do you think we're all crazy? There
are one billion Muslims. It's the most true religion in the world.
Your Christianity's a load of crap. I can find hundreds of
mistakes in the Bible – you say "Christ, son of God." He had
no son . . .'

'You think it's acceptable to say that Christianity's a load of
crap, yet you take offence . . .'

'No. Jesus is our prophet as well. He was our prophet, man.
He had the power to cure the blind . . .'

'You mean it's all right to say the Bible was wrong, but you
still respect Jesus?'

'The Bible is wrong. The Bible was written five hundred
years after Jesus. You have so many verses that are full of
contradictions.'

'And the Qur'an, are there no contradictions there?'

'Prove it! I will debate with you. I'll bring one Islamic scholar.
You can bring a hundred of your priests. But I'm not attacking
your religion. Islam is tolerant. Palestine used to be a Christian
land. Christians, Jews and Muslims lived there peacefully for a
long time. Look what's happened now. Now the Jews are
bashing the Palestinians around.'

I pointed out that the book was breaking all records for the
hardback sales of a difficult literary novel. 'Don't you realise,'
I said, 'that you're helping the author and Penguin to get richer
by this protest? Every person at this demonstration is acting
like a free publicity man. If it hadn't been for the Muslims, the
book would only have sold a few thousand copies.'

The man threw up his hands. 'We Muslim don't think in
materialistic terms like the Jews, you know. You insult us, and
we react. That's been our weakness since the Middle Ages.
We are simple people, but when it comes to the honour of
Islam . . .'

By now the crowd was getting dense. Many people were seated in rows on the grass, preparing for the noontide prayer. On the platform a mullah took over the microphone, and recited the *fatiha*, the opening verses of the Qur'an. Men began praying towards Apsley House, in the direction of Mecca. A group of Shi'as, whose ritual of prayer is subtly different from that of the mainstream Sunnis, formed a separate block behind their turbaned mullah, elegantly cloaked in brown. Facing them was a blown-up photograph of Khomeini, suggestive of heresy: Muslims, like Jews, are forbidden to worship graven images, even of one who claims to represent the Hidden Imam, the messiah of Shi'a eschatology.

Not everyone was praying, however. Many, especially the younger men, continued to mill about in the spring sunshine, mingling with the tourists and onlookers. Few of these non-worshippers were dressed, like their elders, in their traditional Friday best. Instead they wore jeans and headbands, with brightly coloured T-shirts. The most murderous placards were being carried by the non-observant.

The police looked on indifferently while these incitements to murder were paraded, evidently deciding that to arrest the perpetrators would inflame the crowd. They were probably right. The temperature was beginning to rise, the boisterous carnival atmosphere to contain more than a hint of menace. The speeches from the platform did nothing to calm things down. Keith Vaz, Labour MP for Leicester East and a Catholic of Indian origin, pledged to carry on the campaign against *The Satanic Verses* in Parliament. Max Madden, a Bradford MP with a small majority, demanded that Salman Rushdie issue instructions to his publishers to stop printing the book and not to publish the paperback version: 'All of those people who want the people of Britain of all races and all religions to live together in peace and respect and understanding know that *The Satanic Verses* has caused deep offence and threatened the future development of good relations . . .' Then, to cheers and cries of 'Allahu Akbar', he added, in Urdu: 'I know your sadness. I'm fully with you. I fully support you.'

By now the speakers were jostling each other on the platform, squabbling over the microphone. Despite protestations of unity, the clash of sects, and egos, was becoming increasingly obvious. A group of Khomeinists formed a column which pushed its way to the front bearing Ayatollah placards. The policemen and policewomen started to look tense and talked urgently into their portable radios. A group of younger militants moved into Park Lane. Propelled by the Khomeinists they began the march to Downing Street an hour ahead of schedule. The appeals from the platform went unheeded. The main body of demonstrators swept along behind the vanguard. Soon the chanting, placard-waving crowd was pushing its way through Victoria Street and into Parliament Square. Up to this point the police had still managed to maintain a semblance of order; but then the marchers suddenly saw a group of Asian female demonstrators holding aloft a banner proclaiming their membership of Women against Fundamentalism. History does not reveal what taunts or jibes the women threw at the marchers in Urdu, Hindi, Bengali, Pushtu or English. What is certain is that the Muslim psyche was bruised at a tender spot: relations between the sexes. Thereafter the organisers, the stewards and the police lost control. Muslim youths tried physically to assault the erring females. When the police intervened to protect them, they started a running battle: stones, placards, bottles and bits of masonry flew through the air. A dozen police were injured, and a hundred arrests were made, before calm was restored.

Inevitably the scenes of this demonstration, caught by the cameras, confirmed one of the oldest images of Islam: a triumphalist faith of uncompromising masculine supremacy. The God who reveals himself in the Qur'an, the Muslim scripture, eschews the easy personification of his Judaeo-Christian counterpart, being neither Father nor Son. He contains female elements: the twin epithets that adhere to His name, *al rahman*, *al rahim* ('the Merciful, the Compassionate') relate etymologically to the Arabic word for 'womb'. But despite these attributes, the Islamic divinity is seen, primarily, in terms of 'an absolute identity-consciousness with an immutable, eternal and inalienable identity, who is always, significantly, called He.'[2] The Arabian matrix in which Muhammad forged his religion had been a warrior society. Men fought, women bred. The

Qur'an enjoins modesty on both sexes, but is more emphatic in addressing females who are urged to cast down their eyes and to guard their modesty, and not to reveal their adornments except to husbands and close male relatives. Male supremacy is fundamental:

> Men are the managers of the affairs of women, for that God has preferred in bounty one of them over another, and for that they have expended their property. Righteous women are therefore obedient, guarding the secret for God's guarding. And those you fear may be rebellious admonish; banish them to their couches and beat them . . .[3]

According to a tradition the Prophet, who is said to have 'loved women and sweet odours', was less than happy when this particular revelation 'came down': 'I wanted one thing, but God has revealed another thing – and what God has willed must be best,' he is related to have said.[4]

Patriarchy, and the radical polarity of the sexes, is built into the cosmic order as envisioned by the Qur'an. The injunctions to dress modestly, even the beating of recalcitrant wives, may be given liberal interpretations: for example, the translator and commentator Muhammad Asad cites various authorities to the effect that the beating, if done at all, should be merely symbolic, with a folded handkerchief, a toothbrush 'or some such thing'.[5] But the injunction remains, part of the unalterable edifice of God's Word. As does the fact – equally scandalous to a Western sensibility – that in an Islamic court of law a woman's testimony is only worth half a man's.

Whereas Christianity, at least in its Catholic versions, gives some acknowledgement to the female principle in the Virgin, who assimilates the figure of Isis and other pre-Christian deities, the mainstream tradition of Sunni Islam tends to suppress it altogether. There are few female saints and hardly any orders of female Sufis or mystics – at least nothing comparable in terms of scale and organisation to the female religious orders in Christendom. Until recent times, women were positively discouraged from praying in mosques, lest they distract men from their devotions.[6] Islam is the most assertive and androcentric of monotheisms. The Qur'an contains, in the figure of Mary, mother of Jesus, an ideal of womanhood in its submissive aspects: she is the perfect example of *'ubudiyya*, or service to God, which is distinguished by *khilafa*, the principle of vice-regency represented by man. The negative side of the feminine is represented by the terms *musafihat* and *muttakidhat akhdan*, promiscuous women or women who take lovers, 'in other words those women who defy patriarchal controls and feel free to choose how and with whom they have sexual relations.'[7] Any sexual relations, outside the framework of the divine law which allows men up to four wives and the right to initiate divorce by *talaq* or unilateral declaration, are seen as an offence against God punishable by death. Homicide, by contrast, is (with the exception of highway robbery) regarded as a civil tort that can be settled by monetary compensation. Thus where murder is seen as a private matter between families, *zina*, or illicit sexual activity, strikes at the root of patriarchal authority and hence the cosmic order.

To question it is to question the rule of God. *The Satanic Verses* mounted a twofold challenge to the Almighty. By focusing on an alleged incident in the life of the Prophet Muhammad, when Satan is supposed to have interpolated some verses into the scripture, subsequently removed by God, it challenged the absolute authority of the Qur'an, which for most Muslims is literally a part of the Godhead. It did so, like Satan in the story, in the name of the female principle, represented by the pagan goddesses of Mecca, Allat, al-Uzzat and al-Manat. It also seemed to question, from a feminist perspective, the moral integrity of a Prophet whom Muslims revere almost as God, having been their sole channel of communication with the Divine.

Among British Muslims, the great majority of whom come from the Indian subcontinent, the moral underpinning of patriarchy contained in the Qur'an is supplemented by honour, or *izzat*. Where the Qur'anic morality represents an ideal that cannot always be followed, *izzat* makes women the guardians of family pride. Apart from the inequities it canonises in law, the Qur'an demands equal treatment for men and women who fall foul of its strict moral code: the penalty for the adulterer and the adulteress, the fornicator and the fornicatrix – death by stoning – is the same. In practice, however, the rules are difficult to sustain: Islamic law requires that an accusation of *zina* be supported by four independent adult male, or eight female, witnesses – a condition that only the most reckless lovers are likely to satisfy; moreover, an accusation of *zina* which is proven false is punishable by a penalty – eighty lashes – scarcely less severe than *zina* itself. It is *izzat* that serves to sustain and guarantee the sexual double standard. *Izzat* is not seriously affected by the Muslim father who has a beer in the pub or sleeps with a white prostitute (though both these things, of course, are forbidden according to the Qur'an); it is mortally injured by a Muslim girl who discards her virginity before being wed to the man chosen by her parents. In Britain, where Muslims are encouraged to see themselves as a small, embattled minority seeking to preserve their identities against the assimilationist pressures of the wider society, the Qur'an and the figure of the Prophet are deeply implicated in the communal *izzat*. An attack on the sacred text and the person of its revelator, which is what *The Satanic Verses* was seen to be, was experienced as an attack on the honour of the whole community – a community whose collective image of itself, forged in the relatively hostile milieu of the subcontinent, required a greater than average dependence on Muslim shibboleths.

Muslims in the Arab world wear Islam more lightly than their co-religionists in South Asia. The Arab identity is vested in the superiority of language and the historical memory of rulership. Even though the Arab hegemony over Islam lasted only a few centuries, the religion has never entirely broken away from its linguistic matrix. The Qur'an was revealed in Arabic, the tongue of the Arabs. In traditional Islamic theology, moreover, the Qur'an is the Uncreated Word of God – an intrinsic part, as it were, of the Divine Essence. In effect this means, not just that God speaks Arabic, but that the classical Arabic of the Qur'an is a part of the Divine Logos. With such a formidable cultural pedigree, Arabs can afford to be more relaxed than other Muslims about the honour of the Prophet. A perceived attack on the latter will infuriate the pious, and perhaps the *ulema*, the 'learned men' or religious professionals who act as guardians of orthodoxy. But it need not enrage the population at large.

An identity rooted in the fabric of language itself is not so brittle as one whose locus is to be found in a sacred figure (or cow), or a holy text written in a sacred – and largely incomprehensible – language. Indo-Muslim identity, forged in centuries of conflict with the polymorphous expressions of Hindu pantheism, is still unsure of itself: like Jewish identity, it faces the constant threat of losing itself in the cultural mainstream. It thrives on conflict and persecution, for only through such can it reinforce its sense of distinctiveness.

The Satanic Verses, a brilliant, playful, transgressive work that explores and parodies the very ingredients of Indo-British Muslim identity, mixing fact with fiction, history with myth, trod on most of the sensitive spots in this brittle collective ego: the integrity of the Qur'an, the sexuality of the Prophet Muhammad and his wives, the Mothers of the Believers. The majority of the British Muslim community exploded into rage – all, that is, but the tiny portion of it represented by Rushdie and a small Ango-Indian coterie, most of whom had been educated at exclusive institutions where they had become fully assimilated into British society. For that vast majority of British Muslims, unaccustomed to the conventions of contemporary fiction with its rich and varied ingredients, Rushdie's riotous post-modernist pudding proved highly indigestible.

They vomited their fury all over the streets of London, committed solecisms in television studios, enraged the denizens of Fleet Street, Wapping and the Isle of Dogs, and outraged liberals everywhere by demanding that the book be withdrawn, and that the arcane laws of blasphemy be exhumed and extended to cover their faith.

How had these extraordinary scenes come about? How could a mere author, albeit an exceptionally gifted one, fill the streets of London – not to mention Bolton, Blackburn or Bradford – with thousands of demonstrators, many of whom would gladly have hanged him on the spot? Was the outrage genuine, or were Britain's Muslims being manipulated by foreign paymasters in Iran or Saudi Arabia? Could Salman Rushdie, with his Muslim background, have underestimated the impact of his words? Or did he deliberately provoke this rage, in order to focus attention on the many crimes and hypocrisies committed in the name of Islam. Did he know what he was doing? Or was he, despite his literary sophistication, a political *naif*? As an admirer of Rushdie's writing, and a student of Islam, I found these questions acutely interesting. Rushdie did not respond to my request for a telephone interview. Although I was disappointed, his refusal to co-operate allowed me to reach conclusions uninfluenced by anything except his writings and articles about him that appeared in the press. These – rather than Rushdie himself – lie at the centre of the controversy: this is a book, not about an author, but about a book and some of its readers.

CHAPTER ONE

Satanic Fictions

In the radio programme 'Desert Island Discs' celebrity inter-
viewees are invited to choose one book and a luxury item in
addition to the eight records they would like to hear if marooned
on an imaginary atoll. Salman Rushdie appeared on the programme on 8 September 1988 as part of the pre-publication
publicity attending *The Satanic Verses*, his first novel for five
years. Given his Indian Muslim background and his fondness
for fabulous, phantasmagorical narratives, his choice of book
was not surprising: *The Thousand and One Nights*, that great
collection of tales which, as he said, 'contains all other stories'.
His choice of luxury was much more unexpected: 'I would like
to have an unlisted radio telephone,' he said. 'That would allow
me to ring up anybody else, without anyone ringing me.' Not
the least of the many ironies accompanying the Rushdie Affair
is that within six months of that interview Rushdie's wish, in
this regard at least, had been fulfilled. On 16 February 1989,
after the Ayatollah Khomeini had issued a *fatwa* or legal ruling
declaring Salman Rushdie an apostate from Islam and one
whose blood must be shed, the Indo-British novelist and his
wife were obliged to 'go underground' for their own protection.
From the 'safe houses' where armed Special Branch officers are
presumed to guard his person day and night, he can telephone
his agents, publishers, associates and friends with whom he
makes occasional, closely-guarded sorties. They cannot phone
him, and few of them know where he is.

Irony? Or something more uncanny? Irony seems too feeble
a term to apply to the fictions of *The Satanic Verses*. The novel
seems to have overtaken its author, threatening his life and

turning his existence into the kind of nightmarish farce experienced by characters created out of his imagination, characters whose dreams are always leaking out of the vessels of selfhood into the fictional narrative of their lives. The novelist who burlesques the police with hilarious acuity depends for his safety – not to mention company – on the police officers who guard him; the satirist of Thatcherism survives at her government's expense; the champion of the immigrant black or Asian underdog is vilified as a 'racist'; the humorist himself becomes the butt of 'Salman Rushdie' jokes ('What's blonde, has large breasts and lives in Sweden?' 'What did Voyager II find on Jupiter's newly-discovered moon?'); a 'difficult' literary novel, which many people confess to finding unreadable, stays for a year on the bestseller lists, selling more than a million copies in hardback, thanks in large to the campaign against it; the author with high literary ambitions becomes more famous than any other living writer – but at the price of the most precious of all conditions, his personal freedom. Isolated in his 'bunker', he has nothing but an unlisted telephone – and the post – through which to share his triumph with his friends.

The parallels between the events of Rushdie's own life, the fictions he creates, and the order of world events that would presumably run their course without his intervention, seem too apposite to be arbitrary, too loaded with meaning to be dismissed with the 'mere' that usually precedes 'coincidence'. The targets of the satirical invective of his earlier novels – *Midnight's Children* and *Shame* – Indira Gandhi, her son Sanjay, Zulfikar Ali Bhutto and General Zia ul Haqq – all met 'sticky ends'. This overlapping between the 'real' world and Rushdie's fictional universes would be remarkable even without his admission that the conflation of private and public fictions, the realms respectively of art and politics, are central to his project as a writer. 'I think it is a curious phenomenon of the twentieth century,' he told Sue Lawley on 'Desert Island Discs', 'that politicians have got very good at inventing fictions which they tell us as the truth. It then becomes the job of the makers of fiction to start telling the (real) truth.'[1]

Rushdie's perception of political truth has affinities with that of other, mostly Latin American, authors whom the critic

Timothy Brennan groups under the label of 'Third World cosmo-politans'. According to Brennan these writers – including Mario Vargas Llosa, Derek Walcott, Isabel Allende, Gabriel Garcia Marquez and Bharati Mukherjee – have all in their various ways 'supplied sceptical readings of national liberation struggles from the comfort of the observation tower, making that scepticism authoritative'.[2] While mastering the language of the metro-polis, these writers do not become assimilated in a one-sided manner. Being invited to speak as 'Third World' intellectuals they have taken the opportunity to state 'in clear accents that the world is one (not three) and that it is unequal.'[3] In *Midnight's Children* Rushdie satirised the national mythology of India against the backcloth of contemporary sectarian and social ten-sions, with a view to suggesting 'the living presence of India's mythical past, not as "vital tradition", but as false consciousness'.[4] In a different manner, but as part of the same overall fictional enterprise, he lampooned in *Shame* the misuse of Islamic mythology by Pakistan's rulers, Zulfikar Ali Bhutto ('Iskandar Harappa') and General Zia ul Haqq ('Ali Hyder') to sustain their corrupt or tyrannical modes of government.

The fictional form of Rushdie's critique contains an ambiva-lence that has been lacking both in his political journalism and in the political activism in which he was engaged before the Ayatollah Khomeini's death sentence forced him 'under-ground'. In an essay on Orwell he has argued that literature must be political, 'because what is being disputed is nothing less than *what is the case*'.[5] He has been an active and consistent campaigner against racism in Britain: at one time he was in-volved in community relations work for the London borough of Camden. After a visit to Nicaragua in 1986 he gave measured but unequivocal support for the Sandinista government of Daniel Ortega in its struggle against the US-backed Contra rebels.[6]

The political, social and cultural complexities of India are perhaps too great to permit such straightforward partisanship. Rushdie's critique of the self-serving elites of the subcontinent is enfolded in elaborate fictional wrappings, in which form rather than content becomes the vehicle of dissent: as Brennan observes, 'his writing is less in the novels than about them.

Characterisation in any conventional sense barely exists – only a collection of brilliantly sketched cartoons woven together by an intellectual argument.'[7] Like characterisation, metaphor and narrative are perpetually undercut by playful interjections by the author which subvert the suspension of disbelief.

The great religious narratives underpinning the state ideologies of India and Pakistan are woven into the texts of both *Midnight's Children* and *Shame*. The former uses Indian myth to attack 'the political mythmaking' which occurs in Indian politics.[8] At least one Indian critic saw it as written from a Muslim perspective, conveying 'the sensibility of Islamic alienation from the rest of India'.[9] Inevitably, however, religion looms more explicitly in *Shame* than in *Midnight's Children*, religion being the 'glue of Pakistan, holding the halves together; just as consciousness, the awareness of oneself as a homogeneous entity in time . . . is the glue of personality, holding together our then and our now.'[10]

The satire in *Shame* is much more direct and mordant, much less relieved by humour, than in *Midnight's Children*: the work is more deliberately polemical. Its pasteboard characters invite only disgust: indeed the whole novel recalls nothing so much as the crude drawings of Steve Bell, the British radical cartoonist and merciless satirist of Thatcherism. The very concept of Pakistan, 'that fantastic bird of a place, two wings without a body, sundered by the land-mass of its greatest foe, joined by nothing but God'[11] is savaged, along with its ruthless, self-serving rulers who ape the British by using religion to bolster their rule.

Given his views on Pakistan as well as his insistence on challenging the public fictions of politics with private fictions embodying the truths of personal memory and experience, it was perhaps inevitable that in his next novel, *The Satanic Verses*, Rushdie would turn his gaze on the religious mythology of Islam itself. 'Actually one of my major themes is religion and fanaticism,' Rushdie told Madhu Jain of *India Today*. 'I have talked about the Islamic religion because that is what I know the most about. But the ideas about religious faith and the nature of religious experience and also the political implications of religious extremism are applicable with a few variations to just about any religion.'[12]

Rushdie was equally explicit in an interview he gave to Shrabani Basu of the Indian magazine *Sunday*: *The Satanic Verses*, he said, 'is a serious attempt to write about religion and revelation from the point of view of a secular person . . . Besides, Muhammad is a very interesting figure. He's the only prophet who exists even remotely inside history.'[13] This statement – which, incidentally, overlooks a few other prophets 'born inside history' such as Joseph Smith, Baha Ullah, Mary Baker Eddy and L. Ron Hubbard – seemed to contradict his later disclaimer that *The Satanic Verses* wasn't actually *about* Islam, but rather about 'migration, metamorphosis, divided selves, love, death'. The problem for the author, as for the critic, is that the novel encompasses both Islamic origins and migration, the two being indissolubly linked. In the first instance it may have been Rushdie's pre-publication interviews, rather than the book itself, that alerted Islamic activists to the possibility that it would contain material offensive to Muslims – encouraging them to swoop on the offending passages and publicise them. But there is no way in which the controversy could have been avoided.

The Jamaat-i-Islami, the ultra right-wing Islamic party based in Pakistan, had already been targeted by Rushdie in *Shame*. They would certainly have looked for offensive material in the new book, even if its title, *The Satanic Verses*, had been less overtly provocative. Whatever Rushdie's wider attitudes towards Islam, he was evidently quite prepared to do battle with a political faction he saw as reactionary, hostile and inclined to compromise with dictatorship.

Nevertheless, when taken together Rushdie's statements, including the apology he made after the Ayatollah Khomeini issued his *fatwa* condemning him to death, created an impression of ambiguity about his intentions in writing the novel. This is not altogether surprising. The novel, to quote the perceptive American critic Brad Leithauser, 'when taken in its entirety, is so dense a layering of dreams and hallucinations that any attempt to extract an unalloyed line of argument is false to its intention.'[14] It creates a universe of metamorphosis and transformation, in which social and cultural identities lose and recompose themselves in worlds of illusion and dissolution,

where good steals the clothing of evil and the devil masquerades
as God. It is a novel which deliberately sets out to subvert
comfortable moral assumptions.

Its chief protagonists are two Indian actors: Gibreel Farishta,
the flamboyant movie star of numerous Bombay 'theologicals'
who becomes to 'hundreds of millions of believers in that
country in which, to this day, the human population outnum-
bers the divine by less than three to one, the most acceptable
and infinitely recognisable face of the Supreme'[15]; and Saladin
Chamcha – formerly Salahuddin Chamchawala – an urbane
Anglophile who rejects his Bombay background to earn a living
in Britain doing voice-overs for TV commercials, impersonating
packets of crisps, frozen peas, ketchup bottles and such like.

The names of these characters have resonances that are likely
to be missed by the Western reader. Gibreel Farishta translates
literally (from Urdu) into Gabriel Angel – in other words, the
revered figure of the archangel whom Islamic tradition credits
with 'bringing down' the Qur'an from God to Muhammad.
Saladin, of course, is the great champion of medieval Islam who
defeated the Crusaders and restored Sunni Islam to Egypt – a
figure sufficiently admired in medieval Christendom to draw
praise from Dante. 'Chamcha' means 'spoon' in Urdu (hence it
is sometimes anglicised by the urbane Gibreel as 'Spoono'): in
Bombay street argot *chamcha* means something like camp-
follower, groupie or toadie, with homosexual overtones.[16] The
figure of the 'chamcha' occurs in *Midnight's Children* as an image
of those 'leaders whose fortunes [were] built on the miseries of
fleeing Hindu families' after partition in 1947, a class with
which Rushdie appears to identify his own.[17] Gibreel Farishta is
thought, among his other identities, to represent a combination
of the popular Bombay film idol Amitabh Bachan and N. T.
Rama Rao, famous in Indian cinema for his portrayal of mythological beings. In borrowing these real-life figures Rushdie
hardly departs from reality. Like Gibreel in the novel, Bachan
became seriously ill while suffering a freak injury on the set; as
in the novel, all India held its breath while he hovered between
life and death, Mrs Gandhi even cancelling foreign visits in
order to fly to his bedside in Bombay.[18]

The book is constructed out of various interlocking narratives, many of which take place in the dreams of Gibreel. It begins, like the Bible, with a Fall – in this case from an Air India jumbo jet that explodes 30,000 feet above the English Channel after being hijacked by a group of terrorists, led by a fearsome female with more than a passing resemblance to the Goddess Kali. This, too, of course, is based on a real incident – the blowing-up of an Air India Boeing 747 off south-west Ireland in 1985 as a result, it is thought, of a bomb planted by Sikh terrorists in Canada. The two actors fall out of the plane 'like titbits of tobacco from a broken old cigar'. The action is brilliantly realised: a writer with an intensely concrete imagination, Rushdie achieves his surrealist effects with Magritte-like attention to detail: 'Above, behind, below them in the void there hung reclining seats, stereophonic headsets, drinks trolleys, motion discomfort receptacles, disembarkation cards, duty-free video games, braided cups, paper cups, blankets, oxygen masks.'[19]

Gibreel and Saladin miraculously survive, to land softly on a beach in England. Both eventually end up in Ellowen Deeowen, 'a Crusoe-city, marooned on the island of its past, and trying with the help of a Man Friday underclass to keep up appearances.'[20]

After abandoning Chamcha, Gibreel, as befits his archangelic name, acquires a halo which he hides beneath his hat. In Saladin's case, his fall from the aircraft leads to the 'disintegration of a carefully constructed identity'.[21] He turns into a Satanic satyr, half-man, half-goat, with horns, stinking breath, cloven feet and a phallus of monstrous proportions. Their wild, confusing, picaresque adventures form the master plot or 'frame story' around which Rushdie weaves his web of tales. Narrative seems to dissolve into miasmic mists of dreams or fantasy, like a river passing through a mangrove swamp. The structure is as complex, and as confusing to many readers, as that of the Qur'an itself: indeed, *The Satanic Verses*, like its predecessor *Shame*, seems in ways to mirror the Muslim scripture. Like *The Thousand and One Nights*, it is a kind of 'anti-Qur'an' which challenges the original by substituting for the latter's absolutist certainties a theology of doubt.[22]

This theme, linked to the experience of migration, with its loss of certainty and moral absolutism, is central to the controversy generated by the novel. Gita Soghal, supporter of Women against Fundamentalism and member of an immigrant feminist group, the Southall Black Sisters, has made the connection explicit: 'It is in this crisis, where our own orthodoxies have collapsed, that the doubters and transgressors must once more create a space for themselves.'[23] Doubt, of course, infects the fiction as well as its characters: the author spoofs himself, revealing that he has been posing as the Almighty in mobilising the traditional apparatus of divine rage, making wind and thunder shake the room.[24] As the critic Gayatri Spivak has noted, the deity eventually encountered by Gibreel bears a certain resemblance to photographs of Salman Rushdie – a balding, middle-aged man with spectacles and salt-and-pepper beard cropped close to the jaw, who sits on his bed:[25]

> 'Who are you?' he asked with interest . . .
> 'Ooparvala,' the apparition answered. 'The Fellow Up-stairs.'
> 'How do I know you're not the other One,' Gibreel asked craftily, 'Neechayvala, the Guy from Underneath?'[26]

Religious doubt meets *avant-garde* decentring: not only is there 'no clear boundary between religion and fiction as products of the imagination',[27] but the novelist's appropriation of the Creator's function is undermined by constant self-mockery, the 'multiple dreams, carried to absurdity . . . Here is the entire shift from Religion's God to Art's Imagination – a high European theme – played out in the staging of the Author.'[28]

The cast includes a bewildering array of characters, many of whom share the same names as the figures which appear in Gibreel's dreams. Thus Mishal, one of a pair of streetwise Indian sisters living in London, reappears (or is it a different person?) in the sequences that narrate how the Indian prophetess Ayesha, pursued by a cloud of butterflies, leads her followers into the Arabian Sea; while another Ayesha – a prostitute in the mythical city of Jahilia – entertains her clients by taking the role of the Prophet Mahound's favourite wife, in the now notorious brothel scene. Yet another is the evil Empress of Desh, whose overthrow is plotted by the bearded and turbaned Imam-inexile from a rented Kensington flat: there is another touch of prescience here, as the author flirts with danger ('Fiend, the Imam is wont to thunder. Apostate, blasphemer, fraud').[29] The modern-day Mishal's father, Sufyan, the proprietor of the Shandaar café in London, is married to a lady called Hind – the name of the wife of the Prophet Muhammad's leading opponent in Mecca, a figure who in the Jahiliya sequences is given the name Abu Simbel. Other characters, apparently based on real people, have names with suggestive resonances. Billy Battuta, the stammering Indian film producer (based, apparently, on Ismail Merchant) suggests Ibn Battuta, the great Moroccan traveller, and just to confuse things further, a leading character sports the name Rekha Merchant: she is Gibreel's deceased Bombay mistress, who periodically appears on a magic carpet, an avatar possessed with earthy common sense. John Maslama, a deranged Indian Gibreel meets on a train, suggests the 'false' prophet Maslama or Musailima, a contemporary of Muhammad who tried to rouse the Arabian tribes against him; Eugene Dumsday, the American evangelist (based, according to Rushdie, on Duane Gish of the Institute of Creation Research in Southern California) 'gains his freedom by losing his tongue'[30] in the hijack, suggesting a failed prophet of doom.

The sub-plots, set in London or Bombay, satirise, sometimes brilliantly, the modern cosmopolis with its mixture of argots and street language, its cultural hybrids, its seedy immigrant ghettoes: the satire is cool, the characters two-dimensional. The alienations and humiliations of the migrants' world, with its disintegrating and reforming identities, are treated with the flat burlesque of cartoon. Several critics have sensed a lack of empathy in Rushdie's treatment of traditionally disadvantaged groups. Thus Timothy Brennan writes: 'The book's characterisations of West Indians (like its characterisation of women) are often embarrassing and offensive';[31] while Feroza Jussawalla argues that Rushdie's British education makes him 'condescending to all things Indian'.[32] Empathy in fiction, however, comes more readily with the creation of 'rounded' characters: since Rushdie's thesis appears to be that the migrant's experience leads to the discarding and assuming of identities, to create 'rounded' characters would surely be false to his method: his novel's strength lies in its exuberant two-dimensional qualities, its intense visuality, its way with syntax and astonishing lexical range. The shifting of names and characters who dissolve and re-emerge in different guises is matched by a stylistic ingenuity that is breathtaking at times, wearing at others. Sentences lasting a page or more teeter on the brink of collapse; as Brad Leithauser has written, Rushdie 'treats the language as though he owned it'.[33]

It is themes rather than characters that hold the book together; and of its central themes of faith and migration, it is faith – or its loss – that really holds the attention. The religious questions Rushdie raises are serious, even if the treatment is farcical. Religion is part of the immigrant's cultural baggage. To discard it, as many are forced to, at the port of entry, does indeed leave behind a spiritual vacuum, a 'God-shaped hole'.

The Satanic Verses seems the most personal of Rushdie's novels to date, revealing more about his preoccupations with religious faith, love, and cultural identity than any of his earlier works. The two principal characters borrow freely from known events in Rushdie's life. Like Saladin, Rushdie was born in Bombay of well-off parents who packed him off at the age of thirteen to what was then one of Britain's more philistine private boarding schools. Like Saladin, Rushdie, who went to Rugby, was faced at his first school breakfast with the indignity of having to struggle with a kipper while unsympathetic schoolmates looked on, refusing to help. Rushdie says he hated Rugby. For one thing, he suddenly discovered that he was 'an Indian': 'There are no Indians in India,' he explained to Gerald Marzorati. 'There are classes, of course, and regional identifications. Here in England it is largely understood as a race – and at the schoolboy level, back then, that was no fun.'[34] Rushdie says he never really made a friend at Rugby. He felt he was triply disadvantaged: bad at games, good at his studies, and foreign. Rugby was one of those schools where an inverted value system applied to academic work: if you were good at it, you must be 'wet'. Though pale-skinned, he was subject to racial slurs.

In *The Satanic Verses* Rushdie's first kipper becomes a comic metaphor for England's impenetrable social code: 'England was peculiar-tasting smoked fish full of spikes and bones, and nobody would ever tell him how to eat it.' Many other autobiographical elements find their way into the novel. Like Saladin, Rushdie appears to have had a difficult relationship with his father, Anis Ahmed Rushdie, a Cambridge-educated businessman with literary tastes who, according to Rushdie, inherited 'quite a lot of money and spent the rest of his life losing it'.[35] Like Saladin, Rushdie married a beautiful young Englishwoman with an upper-class voice – though (judging from one telephone conversation) a voice considerably more cultivated than the Sloane Ranger bray burlesqued in the book, 'composed of tweeds, headscarves, summer pudding, hockey-sticks, thatched houses, saddle-soap, house-parties, nuns, family pews, large dogs and philistinism [which] in spite of all her attempts to reduce its volume was loud as a dinner-jacketed drunk throwing bread-rolls in a club.'[36]

Rushdie's first wife was Clarissa Luard: Saladin's estranged spouse is Pamela Lovelace, a name which combines Richardson's earlier heroine with the tormentor of his later novel *Clarissa*. The book is full of such references to English, Urdu and Latin American literatures, which readers find ingenious or irritating, according to taste. Rushdie is massively well-read and likes to display his learning. Saladin's career in advertising draws on Rushdie's own knowledge of the profession – based on his early years as a part-time copywriter for Ogilvy and Mather. Rushdie claims to have made up the slogan 'naughty but nice' for cream buns, though this has been disputed by some, who say the phrase first occurred in a music hall song: the phrase, however, is not so unusual as to preclude independent gestations.

The novel also draws on Rushdie's wide experience in the theatre, cinema and television. At Cambridge, where Rushdie found his level much more successfully than at Rugby, he took part in both the straight theatre and in the satirical Footlights, a seedbed for British talent since the early 1960s. 'I was a tiny bulb in the Footlights,' he says; but he was sufficiently interested in the theatre to join a radical company, the Oval Theatre in Kennington, after graduating from Cambridge. He sought to become an actor, partly as a fall-back position in case he did not 'make it' as a writer. Although he had wanted to be a writer from an early age, he was terrified of discovering that he lacked the ability.[37] His technique as a novelist owes much to the theatre, as Mark Lawson has noted: 'In the writer he became, it is possible to see the actor he was . . . Rushdie is a verbal impresario, using the page as a stage, hurrying characters in and out, raising and lowering drapes, himself at the centre, swirling phrases like a cape. He points out that, in Indian theatre and dance, performer and creator are generally the same.'[38]

In *The Satanic Verses* theatricality is personified by Gibreel, the extrovert, flamboyant Bombay superstar whose psychotic dreams carry so much of the novel's explosive theological material. A man of Rushdie's accomplishments invites envy, and it is a mark of his sense of humour – as well as what his detractors might see as a titanic, not to say cosmic, egotism – that Gibreel comically displays some of the characteristics that have made Rushdie less than universally popular in the kipperish world of London society, where talent is expected to be modest about itself and stars are supposed to keep their egos (like well-bred dogs, horses, and children) under control.

What strikes one most, however, is the consistency of Rusdie's commitment. A less determined man might have been put off by the failure of *Grimus*, his first novel, a fantasy that draws on Sufi themes. Undeterred, Rushdie left his job in advertising to write *Midnight's Children* which won the Booker Prize in 1984. His disappointment at failing to win it a second time with *Shame* was visible even to those who watched the presentation on television. His ambition, it is said, is such that even if he won the Nobel Prize, he would not be content until he had won it twice. Rushdie incurred some criticism when he left his editor, Liz Calder, who had recognised his talent early on, had stuck with him after the failure of *Grimus*, through the triumph of *Midnight's Children* and *Shame*, fully expecting that *The Satanic Verses* would adorn the list of Bloomsbury, the independent company she helped to form after leaving Tom Maschler at Cape.

The facts behind this, however, need not necessarily reflect badly on Rushdie: many authors change agents or publishers; most are interested in getting the largest possible advances for their books. The £50,000 allegedly offered by Bloomsbury for the UK hardback rights for *The Satanic Verses* was hardly commensurate with his standing as one of the half dozen most gifted young writers in the English language. What upset some people in the literary community was the manner of his departures, his style of doing things.

Gibreel shares quite a few of his creator's characteristics, even physical ones: his face 'reduced to life size, set amongst ordinary mortals . . . stood revealed as oddly un-starry. Those low-slung eyelids . . . something coarse about the nose, the mouth too well-fleshed to be strong.'[39] 'The worst thing about him,' Gibreel's lover, Allie Cone, tentatively concludes, is 'his genius for thinking himself slighted, belittled, under attack'.[40] But it is the inner life of Gibreel, the quest for love, the loss of religious faith that seems to echo gleanable facts of Rushdie's experience. 'There's a hole inside me where God used to be,' Rushdie told Gerald Marzorati. 'I am no longer an observant Muslim and I wanted to explore this hole. And of course, that's what novels do, isn't it? Explore.'[41]

Though the treatment is comic, these psychic explorations follow a tragic progression through loss of faith, rejection in love and eventual suicide. Like Rushdie, Gibreel learns the stories about the Prophet and the origins of Islam from his mother's knee; he comes across the incident of the Satanic Verses in which the devil is related to have inserted a sentence in the Qur'an, subsequently abrogated, which plants in him the seed of religious doubt. Rushdie encountered this incident while researching a paper he wrote at Cambridge on the early history of Islam. This and other episodes from the story of the Prophet's life which subsequently appear transmogrified in Gibreel's dreams cast doubt on the Islamic orthodoxy that the Qur'an was transmitted without any editing by Muhammad.

In the novel Gibreel's loss of faith is linked with his obsessive, destructive relationship with the female climber and explorer Allie Cone, a cool, tough blonde whose 'skin possessed the colour and translucency of mountain ice'.[42] The affair, it has been suggested, mirrors Rushdie's own passionate involvement with the Australian travel-writer and novelist Robyn Davidson.[43] According to a friend who was close to them both, 'It's awful when people bring out the most negative aspects in each other.

When they parted, he was utterly devastated. Afterwards Rushdie married the American novelist Marianne Wiggins, to whom *The Satanic Verses* is dedicated. She shared his ordeal for several months, moving from one safe house to another every two or three nights. However, the strain of this peripatetic incarceration evidently proved too severe. In August 1989 Wiggins announced that she and her husband were living apart.

In the novel the relationship between Gibreel and Allie is a major thread in the weave of narratives, binding its emotional and religious themes together. Allie appears in his life at the moment Gibreel crosses the Rubicon of religious doubt in the classic manner of Jewish rebels, by stuffing himself with pork and discovering that retribution is not instantaneous:

> 'Don't you get it?' he shouted after her, spewing sausage fragments from the corners of his mouth. 'No thunderbolt. That's the point.'
>
> She came back to stand in front of him. 'You're alive,' she told him. 'You got your life back. *That's* the point.'[44]

For a time Allie, the climber of Everest, where land attempts to 'metamorphose into sky', fills the God-shaped hole inside Gibreel. It is after Allie throws him out that he begins to hallucinate in earnest as he accelerates towards a complete schizophrenic breakdown, the earlier nightmares of his 'archangelic other self' leaking into, and eventually overwhelming, his waking personality. The psycho-drama is handled in comic picaresque: something between the magical realism of Gunter Grass's *Tin Drum* and the urbane comic Englishness with which Evelyn Waugh described his own hallucinatory experiences in *The Ordeal of Gilbert Pinfold*.

Gibreel dreams his 'archangelic' other self, as revelator of the Qur'an, bearer of God's Message to mankind. The link between these deeply transgressive dreams and the Gibreel–Cone affair is effected through unconscious etymologies or 'Joycean slips' of the kind that occur in *Finnegans Wake*: the Prophet Mahound (as Crusading demonologists knew Muhammad) receives his revelations on Mount Cone (Mount Hira in Islamic tradition): Allie's surname, anglicised from Cohen, the Hebrew priest, shares the same semitic root as the Arabic *kahin* or soothsayer, which was what many of Muhammad's contemporaries of the *jahiliya*, the 'period of ignorance' before the coming of Islam, assumed the Prophet to be. The place of revelation bears the name of the beloved. The collapse of religious certainty symbolised by the affair of the Satanic Verses mirrors the betrayal experienced by Gibreel in his waking life, as he becomes increasingly, obsessively jealous. Saladin acts the part of Iago to Gibreel's Othello, using the thousand-and-one voices of his advertising days in a campaign of obscene telephone calls.

In Gibreel's dreams the cracks of doubt revealed by the Satanic Verses open the floodgates of unbelief. The brothel called The Curtain, where prostitutes act out the part of the Prophet Mahound's wives, is the anti-mosque where the ultimate transgressive fantasies of the faithless Jahilites are performed. The character at the centre of this section is the poet Baal, Salman's drinking companion and unreconstructed pagan, who finds refuge in the brothel, where he pretends to be a eunuch. Baal seems endowed, like Rushdie, with a certain uncanny prescience: 'A poet's work,' he tells Abu Simbel, the Grandee of Mecca who employs him, is 'to name the unnameable, to point at frauds, to take sides, start arguments, shape the world and stop it from going to sleep. And if rivers of blood flow from the cuts his verses inflict, then they will nourish him.'[45] At least twenty-one people were to die in the anti-Rushdie agitation, nineteen of them in the Indian subcontinent, two in Belgium.

The Satanic Verses has a strong feminist undercurrent which surfaces in the brothel scene, where whores take the part of the Prophet's wives. The clients circulate in its innermost courtyard around the Fountain of Love, 'much as the pilgrims rotated for other reasons around the ancient Black Stone'. The anti-mosque appears to be a Swiftean inversion of the attitudes to women legitimised by the Prophet's numerous marriages. 'The fifteen-year-old whore "Ayesha" was the most popular with the paying public, just as her namesake was with Mahound . . .'[46] The girls all marry Baal who becomes, as it were, the anti-Prophet. Salman visits his old friend and drunkenly relays gossip from the Prophet Mahound's camp:

'Gibreel had recited verses giving [Mahound] full divine support. God's own permission to fuck as many women as he
liked.'[47] Muslim apologists rationalise the Prophet's twelve
wives – eight in excess of the four permitted to ordinary Muslims
– in terms of his need to form political and tribal alliances (an
argument paradoxically put forward by Baal in the novel). The
annals written long before ideological defensiveness afflicted
Muslim writers tell a different story: next to prayer, the Prophet
'loved women and sweet odours': the great Andalusian Sufi
mystic, Ibn ul Arabi, erected a whole theosophical edifice
around this phrase. Muhammad's fondness for women, and
the attraction he held for them, was part of his aura as a prophet,
as one specially chosen by God. Like Joseph Smith, the Mormon
prophet, Muhammad may have justified his sexual urges by
reference to divine revelation.[48] The brothel scene is the most
deliberately iconoclastic in the book. It flirts with danger in a
manner that yields more than irony, given Rushdie's current
predicament. It is Baal's idea to dress up the whores as the
'Mothers of the Faithful':

> How many wives? Twelve, and one old lady, long dead. How
> many whores behind The Curtain? Twelve again; and, secret
> on her black-tented throne, the ancient Madam, still defying
> death. Where there is no belief, there is no blasphemy. Baal
> told the Madam of his idea; she settled matters in her voice
> of a laryngitic frog. 'It's very dangerous,' she pronounced,
> 'but it could be damn good for business. We will go carefully,
> but we will go.'[49]

Like almost everything else in *The Satanic Verses*, the brothel
scene has its literary pedigree: in this case there seems more
than a whiff of Genet's *Le Balcon*. But there is no doubting that
the author knows that he is being dangerously transgressive:
after Baal is finally discovered in the brothel, the Prophet
Mahound himself issues a *fatwa*: the impious poet is sentenced
to beheading. Baal remains defiantly unrepentant: 'within the
hour, and as soldiers manhandled him out of the tent towards
the killing ground, he shouted over his shoulder: "Whores
and writers, Mahound. We are the people you can't forgive."

Mahound replied, "Writers and whores. I see no difference here."[50]

It has been necessary for the purpose of this book to focus on the areas that Muslims have found most offensive. In addition to the passages already mentioned, Muslim readers have generally taken exception to epithets like 'bastard', 'scum', 'goons', 'bums', 'fucking clowns' being attached – always in Gibreel's dreams – to such revered figures as Abraham and the Prophet's Companions, including Bilal, Khalid and Salman. Just as the wider fictional context of Gibreel's dreams is usually ignored, so is the fact that most of these epithets are placed in the mouths of Mahound's arch-enemy, Abu Simbel (Abu Sufyan in history) and Abu Simbel's satirist Baal: as Denis MacEoin points out, even Ibn Ishaq, the chief source for the life of the Prophet, puts epithets such as 'fools, blockheads, louts' into the mouths of his Qurayshite enemies.[51]

It would be wrong, however, to see the novel exclusively in terms of its Islamic preoccupations. The most consistent theme that can be extrapolated from Rushdie's baroque elaborations of plot and character concerns the transformations of identity that affect the migrant who leaves his homeland, with its familiar reference points and cultural certainties, to find himself in a milieu where the rules are different and all the moral reference points have been changed.

The migrant's dilemma – to change, risking loss of faith and identity, or to try to hold on to a consistent idea of selfhood – lies at the novel's heart, and provides its unexpectedly touching conclusion. It is Saladin Chamcha, the 'creature of selected discontinuities, a willing re-invention of himself', who, by watching his father die in what is a remarkably moving, yet clear-eyed description, recovers his former, unassimilated, selfhood as Salahuddin Chamchawala, the Bombay bourgeois; it is Gibreel, the 'untranslated man' whom the world considers 'good' for wishing to remain 'continuous', who is finally destroyed, unable to contain the eruption of a religious megalomania which leaks into and overwhelms his waking self, 'making him that angelic Gibreel he has no desire to be'.[52] The dilemmas of identity and religious doubt are resolved through filial love.

Though the treatment is comic, the questions posed by *The Satanic Verses* are serious and pertinent. How does the believer in any religion distinguish between the Voice of God and the Devil's promptings? Was the Prophet deceived, or was he not? What about those who act and speak in his name? Where hundreds of thousands have been tortured, murdered or sent to their deaths in the name of Islam, it is entirely legitimate to probe its origins, question its claims to truth. What seems more questionable is the savage coarseness of tone that occurs in the brothel scene.

Is this intended to be gratuitously insulting to the Prophet's memory, as outraged Muslims insist, or is it an imaginative way of charting the migrant's path from faith to scepticism, his shifting perspective of women, his attempts to exorcise childhood archetypes? Because of what has happened, it has become impossible to read these passages without hindsight, without the knowledge that, directly or otherwise, their appearance in print has led to the loss of twenty-one human lives, and that by a preposterous form of retribution, Rushdie has been given a life sentence for writing them. That awareness leaks into the reader's consciousness – that reader, at least, who is remotely aware of Islamic sensitivities, of the devotion Muslims have towards their sacred myths. Just as Gibreel's dreams spill over into his waking reality, Rushdie's fictions seem to leak like acid from a battery into that other, 'real' world of flesh and blood that acts out its dreams and fantasies before television cameras manned by real technicians.

The rage with which this extraordinary, challenging novel has been greeted by Muslims in Britain and beyond proves that Rushdie has touched upon some very raw nerves in a community experiencing the very insecurities and dilemmas he portrays. It is difficult to believe that, given his knowledge of Indian Muslim cultures and values, he was unaware of the impact his book would make. So many passages seem to flirt with the fate that subsequently engulfed the book and its author. More than any other living writer, his fiction seems to possess a life of its own: as Peter van den Veer neatly observes, 'Rushdie's magic realism makes a raid on reality, but reality hits back with a raid on fiction.'[53]

CHAPTER TWO

Honour and Shame

'We Muslims are a tolerant people but we cannot bear insult.' Such was the gist of several conversations I had with Muslims about *The Satanic Verses* both before and after Khomeini issued his notorious *fatwa*. Even Dr Zaki Badawi, head of the Muslim College in Ealing and one of Britain's most liberal Muslim leaders, felt deeply pained by the book: 'What he has written is far worse to Muslims than if he had raped one's own daughter,' he told the *Guardian*. 'Muslims seek Mohammed as an ideal on whom to fashion our lives and conduct, and the Prophet is internalised into every Muslim heart. It's like a knife being dug into you – or being raped yourself.'[1] The Tanzanian scholar Dr Ali Mazrui told an audience at Cornell University that his Pakistani friends had likened the book to a kind of child abuse in reverse: 'It's as if Rushdie had composed a brilliant poem about the private parts of his parents, and then gone to the market place to recite that poem to the applause of strangers, who invariably laughed at the jokes he cracks about his parents' genitalia – and he's taking money for doing it.'[2]

The sexual imagery is significant, revealing the essential connection between faith and purity, and more especially the purity of women. As Marina Warner has pointed out in the Christian context, 'characterising the offence in the language of sexual outrage connects with the repressions of Catholicism, because the history of the Church's authority is very often bound up with the proclamation of the necessary purity of women, especially with the virginity of Mary, the Mother of God.'[3] The Virgin is revered in Islam, though not as an object of worship. She has no powers of intercession, and she is the mother of a prophet, not of God.

However, the connection between faith and sexuality is, if anything, even more entrenched in Islamic cultures than others. Qur'anic epistemology divides the world between the realms of the revealed or exoteric (*al shahada* or *al zahir*) on the one hand and that of the hidden or esoteric (*al ghaib* or *al batin*) on the other. The latter is known fully only to God, but knowledge of it is possessed by sheikhs and other holy men who may divine the hidden meanings of scripture and of life itself.

'Righteous women are therefore obedient, guarding the secret (*al ghaib*) for God's guarding . . .'[4] Muhammad Asad translates *al ghaib* in this Qur'anic passage as 'intimacy', a word which suggestively links the divine with the sexual. Sexuality, as the anthropologist Michael Gilsenan explains, may be closely related to the 'hidden' or secret realm signified by *al ghaib*. 'It is central to every member of the society at the level of personal identity, as a member of a social group, and of a whole culture that formulates and proscribes certain strict conceptions of rules and sanctions for sexual behaviour and of the reproduction of society through its "proper" conduct . . .'[5] The mind – body distinction that produces the Manichean division in Augustinian Christianity between body and soul, flesh and spirit, is absent from the Qur'an: the word *nafs*, for example, means both self and soul. Celibacy is condemned in a number of *hadiths* such as 'There is no monkery in Islam'; marriage is extolled, being enjoined on the believers as the better part of faith.

In this most patriarchal of religions sexual transgressions – the sin of *zina* or fornication – are crimes against God, punishable by death. Certain categories of homicide, by contrast, are merely torts, civil offences to be settled by the payment of compensation. In essence, though marriage is not a sacrament as in Christianity, there exists a fusion of the sexual and the sacred in Islam that is all the more powerful because it reinforces a social code rooted in Mediterranean and Asian values of honour and shame.

None of this would of itself be adequate to explain the force of the Muslim reaction against Rushdie's novel: but a moment's reflection suggests that any association between sexual impropriety and the Prophet Muhammad makes a highly combustible mix. The Muhammad who is lodged in the Muslim psyche is not the same as the Muhammad of history. Pious Muslims have occasionally taken offence at the treatment of the latter by such writers as Montgomery Watt, Michael Cook, and Maxime Rodinson,[6] but knowledge of these works among Muslims at large has been limited; in any case, the writings of these and other orientalists tends to be framed in the polite language of academic discourse. Rushdie's language, by contrast, is the language of the street. Appropriate though it may be to the milieu of his deracinated migrants, it deliberately jars a Muslim sensibility brought up to nurture the figure of a prophet safely cocooned in the realm of *al ghaib*. The blasphemy perceived here concerns manner rather than substance: in seeking to rescue his 'Mahound' from the hell to which Christian polemicists had consigned him, Rushdie enters the sacral space Muhammad occupies in Muslim feeling and affection. That entry is perceived as a violation, as a kind of 'rape'.

Modern-day Muslims object to being called 'Muhammadans' on the ground that they do not worship their prophet as Christians worship Christ. While this is theologically correct, in reality the reverence accorded the Prophet in many traditions is only a degree below deification. This is particularly true of the Muslim communities of the Indian subcontinent, the principal source of the campaign against *The Satanic Verses* until Khomeini issued his famous *fatwa*.

In the Qur'an the Prophet explicitly disclaims (or rather, is told by God to disclaim) any supernatural powers that might lead the faithful to worship him rather than the divine author of the Qur'an:

Say: 'I have no power to profit for myself, or hurt, but as God will. Had I knowledge of the Unseen I would have acquired much good, and evil would not have touched me. I am only a warner, and a bearer of good tidings, to a people believing.'[7]

The injunction not to worship the Prophet, however, has tended to be honoured in the breach. The veneration of his person is accompanied by the usual repertoire of miraculous legends that surround sacred figures in popular cultures. A divine aura settled on his father just before his conception.[8] Angels attended his birth; during his childhood they opened his breast and cleansed his heart of all sin.[9] Annemarie Schimmel has demonstrated how deeply the veneration of the Prophet is ingrained in Islamic cultures, especially in the Indian subcontinent, where for reasons of language the Qur'an is less accessible.

In the Islamic literary tradition, Muhammad's moral perfections are matched by his physical beauty and the absence of all physical impurities. He was born fully circumcised.[10] The earth swallowed up his excrement[11]; more acceptable body products like hairs and nail-clippings were collected as talismans.[12] His shirt was enough to cure a Jew's blindness; the fragrance of his presence was such that it left its beautiful odour of musk around those to whom he appeared in dreams (and that, of course, included just about anyone with serious claims to holiness).[13] His footprint, preserved from his miraculous Night Journey to Jerusalem, is still venerated in the Dome of the Rock.[14] Like the Night Journey, the story of another popular miracle – the Splitting of the Moon – has its origin in an otherwise obscure Qur'anic phrase, *inshaq al qamar* ('the moon has split'). Even in early traditions this is explained, not as a reference to the cosmic cataclysms of the Day of Judgement, but in terms of a miracle performed by the Prophet to convince the doubting Meccans: he split the moon with his finger, and between the two halves Mount Hira could be seen. The legend became a favourite with mystically-inclined poets: the believer knows, sings Rumi, that one who is devoted to the Prophet 'splits the moon with Mustafa's (the Chosen One's) finger'.[15]

Despite the limitations of formal theology, the figure of Muhammad in the mystical literature aspires to godhood in a manner barely inferior to Christ. The Light of Muhammad – a neo-platonist idea that finds its Qur'anic anchoring in the Sura of Light, the Night Journey[16] and other mystical passages – pre-existed in eternity. In the image of the Sufi Sahl al Tustari

(d. 896) the origin of this light in pre-eternity is 'depicted as a luminous mass of primordial adoration in the presence of God which takes the shape of a transparent column . . . and constitutes Muhammad as the primal creation of God.'[17] At the beginning of creation, God 'created Adam from the light of Muhammad'.[18] 'I was a prophet,' says Muhammad in one *hadith*, 'while Adam was still between water and clay'[19] – that is to say, he is 'uncreated', like the Qur'an.

Later mystics and poets would elevate the primordial Muhammad to a position scarcely distinguishable from that of the Divine Logos in Christianity. In the system of Ibn al Arabi, the famous Andalusian mystic, Muhammad becomes *al insan al kamil*, the perfect man or 'pupil in the eye of humanity', prototype of the universe as well as of the individual. Thus Ibn al Arabi's follower Abdul Karim al Jili rhapsodises:

O Centre of the compass! O inmost ground of truth!
O pivot of necessity and contingency!
O eye of the entire circle of existence! O point of the
  Qur'an . . .
Thou art transcendent, nay thou art immanent, nay thine
  is all that is known and unknown, everlasting and
  perishable.
Thine in reality is Being and not-being . . .[20]

At the more popular level mystical hyperbole filters down into the less philosophical images of love found in Urdu poetry:

Muhammad Mustafa is the colour of the rose of Love,
And his curls are the spring of the hyacinths of love,
Certainly he, he alone, is the most radiant sun of Love,
and through him are illuminated the luminous stars of
  Love.[21]

The pious men of the cities, known as 'Hadith Folk', condemned the mystical adoration of the Prophet as a form of *shirk* or idolatry, the 'association' of lesser beings with God. However, mainstream Sunni Islam was involved in a 'Muhammadolatry' of its own that was hardly less extravagant. From the earliest times pious Sunnis – and not just those of a mystical orientation – had gone to great lengths to model their lives on that of the Prophet.

Every detail of his life, down to the cut of his beard, the clothes he wore, the food he liked, became in the formative period of Islamic culture (the eighth and ninth centuries CE) the ideal for a whole civilisation. Those who sought merit in supererogation avoided what the Prophet avoided. Some eschewed mangoes, or melons, because there was no record that the Prophet had eaten them; others foreswore garlic, even though there was no taboo, because the Prophet was reported to have hated it. They loved honey, mutton and cats, because he loved honey, mutton and cats. Generally Muhammad's followers emphasised precept before doctrine, orthopraxis before orthodoxy. And the heart of praxis was the example of the Prophet himself. Thus the greatest medieval theologian, al Ghazali (d. 1111) – sometimes thought of as the Aquinas of Islam – wrote in his massive *Ihya ulum al din* ('Revival of the Religious Sciences'):

> Know that the key to happiness is to follow the *sunna* (lit. 'path') and to imitate the Messenger of God in all his coming and going, his movements and rest, in his way of eating, his attitude, his sleep and his talk. I do not mean this (just) in regard to religious observance, for there is no reason to neglect the traditions which were concerned with this aspect. I rather mean all the problems of custom and usage, for only by following them unrestricted succession is possible. God has said: 'Say: If you love God, follow me, and God will love you' (Sura 3:29), and He has said: 'What the messenger has brought – accept it, and what he has prohibited, refrain from it!' (Sura 59:7) That means, you have to sit while putting on trousers, and to stand when winding a turban, and to begin with the right foot when putting on shoes . . .[22]

Muhammad's conduct, elaborated through a myriad of anecdotes, became the absolute model for Muslim life. The smallest details of his behaviour became examples to be emulated. 'The prophet taught us everything, from prayer to defecation' went a well-known saying. Muhammad is, like Islam itself, a social fact, an archetype or role-model lodged in the psyche of the masses, an integral aspect of Muslim identity. An assault on his reputation is perceived as an assault on the Muslim personality.

Rushdie's use of the name for the Prophet who appears as Mahound in Gibreel's dreams challenges, or perhaps exorcises, this mythic archetype lodged in the Muslim psyche. Mahound – with his variants Mahum, Mahun, Mahoune, Macon, Machound and so forth – is a medieval European version of Muhammad, whom Christians presumed the infidel Muslims worshipped as God. For poets from Langland to Burns, Mahound is synonymous with the devil – an expletive by which people swear, or a false god.[23] The image of the prophet-as-devil came to Europe with the returning Crusaders; its origins lie in the polemics that followed the Muslim conquest of the Near East, when disgruntled Christian clerics put it about that the Prophet of Islam was an impostor who had learned his devilish craft from a disillusioned Greek monk who was determined to destroy the Church. The figure of the devilish Prophet of Islam was taken into Protestant demonology, where it was assimilated to those of the Pope and Anti-Christ as demonic agencies. Thus a tract by Humphrey Prideaux, Dean of Norwich, entitled *The True Nature of the Imposture Fully Displayed by the Life of Mahomet* (1718) assures the good dean's readers that 'Mahomet began the Imposture about the same time that the Bishop of Rome' set out to destroy mankind – the two impostors being, as it were 'the two feet of Antichrist'; while the Reverend George Bush, first Professor of Hebrew and Oriental languages at New York University, a forebear of the current President of the United States, explained in his *Life of Mohammed* how the Prophet of Islam 'meditated and matured the bold design of palming a new religion upon the world'.[24]

The Muhammad of the Crusaders was a charlatan, a madman, a lustful sensualist who met with a sticky end. The supposed revelations he received came to him in the course of epileptic fits ('He broke out into such madness,' wrote William of Tyre in the thirteenth century, 'that he dared to lie that he was a prophet, that he was sent by God . . .').[25] In a stark contradiction of his actual role as preacher of the most uncompromising of all monotheisms, he is claimed to have taught the Saracens to worship idols: indeed one of the meanings listed under Mahound in the *Oxford English Dictionary* is 'idol'. He is presumed to have used the wives of other men to satisfy his lusts and to 'generate more Prophets', justifying his actions by revelation, then erecting them into general laws for the benefit of his followers.[26] His death was variously attributed to a beautiful Jewess who poisoned the leg of lamb she served him; or to an even worse fate – being torn to death by pigs while in a drunken stupor ('Since he taught uncleanness and shame,' wrote Gerald of Wales, 'it was by pigs, which are unclean animals, that he was devoured'[27]).

Though the figure of Mahound in *The Satanic Verses* falls short of the medieval stereotype, Rushdie's invocation of this name is, to put it mildly, highly provocative – at least for an educated Muslim sensibility, one sufficiently cognizant of Western literature to be aware of the name's historical baggage. Given that the authorial voice is ambiguous, prone to undermining itself, the claimed motive of rehabilitation – 'To turn insults into strengths, whigs, tories, Blacks all chose to wear with pride the names they were given in scorn'[28] – sounds unconvincing. Thus it is that Feroza Jussawalla, taking issue with Edward Said, attacks 'the mimicry of modernism behind which Rushdie chooses to veil his real political affiliations.' Brushing aside Rushdie's celebrated critique of the British nostalgia for empire, evidenced in the popularity of the television adaptation of Paul Scott's Raj Quartet and David Lean's film version of *A Passage to India*, she argues that his attitude is really neo-colonialist, inspired by his British education. 'Did he forget,' she asks, 'that the Muslims of Brick Lane and Bradford would be as much irradiated by history as he is?'[29] For those rooted in the culture of veneration, with its naïve celebration of childhood archetypes, the name Mahound is of itself insulting. The system of honour, *izzat*, ever sensitive to insult, ensures that even the least educated receive the message that Mahound is a racist label. A more traditional style of fiction – one which sustained the suspension of disbelief instead of undermining it – might have placed Satanic thoughts in the head of a villain and got away with it.

All religions mix fact with fiction, and in this respect Islam is no different from Christianity. Historical studies of the origins of Islam range from an extreme scepticism which questions the very existence of the Prophet as an historic figure to the total credulity of the orthodox Muslim believer. As a saboteur not only of religious certainties, but of the quasi-certainties of conventional fictional illusion, Rushdie revels in shaking up the box in which fact lies concealed in its mythical wrappings.

If religion is permitted to mix fact with fantasy, why not fiction? This argument has been largely ignored by Rushdie's Muslim critics, who find it easier to attack his insolence than to address the serious questions about religious 'truth' and 'falsehood' he raises. The origins of Islam are, in fact, too opaque to make it possible to determine with any precision what really happened in seventh-century Arabia and what was invented by pious minds in subsequent generations. The original story of the Satanic Verses, from which Rushdie takes his title, is a case in point.

The story is related by two of the early Muslim commentators, Tabari and Ibn Sa'd. In Tabari's version, the incident occurred soon after Muhammad began his mission in Mecca. When he saw that the Meccans were rejecting his doctrine of the single God, he was overcome with the desire to make it easier for them to accept it. After giving utterance to the revelation preserved in the Qur'an as part of Surat al-Najm ('The Star')[30] – 'Have you considered al-Lat, al-'Uzza and Manat, the third the other', a reference to three female tribal deities – Satan put upon his tongue the following words: 'These are the exalted *gharaniq* [swans or cranes, i.e. beautiful ladies] whose intercession is to be hoped for.' On hearing this, the Meccans were delighted, for it suggested that Muhammad had accepted their beloved goddesses as worthy of worship. When Muhammad prostrated himself, they all did likewise. The news of this great reconciliation, which healed the bitter divisions in the Meccan community that had resulted from Muhammad's preaching, reached the Muslims who had gone to Abyssinia to avoid persecution, inspiring their premature return to Mecca. But then the angel

Gibreel came to Muhammad and showed him his error. God
replaced the Satanic Verse with that which is now in the text.
'Why – for yourselves [you would choose only] male offspring,
whereas to Him [you assign] female . . .'[31] The meaning of this
verse is as follows: since the Meccan polytheists were in the
habit of killing their female offspring, a practice vigorously
condemned in the Qur'an, it was illogical as well as impious of
them to ascribe daughters to God and to worship them as divine
beings.[32]

The story was dismissed by some of the early authorities on
the ground that the chain of transmitters (*isnad*) linking it to the
Prophet Muhammad was weak: indeed, it was considered too
unreliable to allow the story to be included in any of the six
authoritative collections of *hadiths* or Traditions assembled in
the centuries after Muhammad's death. The methodology of
the *hadith* collectors depended more on *isnads* than content. A
hadith is rather like the provenance with which an art dealer
supplies a painting, tracing it back to the artist's studio through
a chain of owners. Thus a typical *hadith* will be prefixed with
an *isnad* that goes something like this: 'A heard from B who
heard from C who heard from D who heard it from Abu Hureira
(an authority who figures in many *isnads*) who heard it from
Aisha (the Prophet's youngest wife, and the source of many
hadiths) who relates that the Prophet always cleaned his teeth
with a stick.' The *hadith* collectors paid enormous attention to
the character and reliability of the various links in the chain of
transmitters. Western scholars, however, have pointed out that
they paid much less attention to content: in particular Ignaz
Goldziher, the founder of modern Western *hadith* studies, argued that despite the methodology of the *hadith* collectors, a
great many anachronisms found their way into the canonised
collections. Most Muslim scholars defend the traditional
methodology; some modernists and reformers, however, have
put forward arguments very similar to Goldziher's, insisting
that the only reliable source of law and practice is the Qur'an
itself.[33]

The story of the Satanic Verses is still controversial. Many
modern Muslim writers regard it as 'apocryphal gossip' [34]
dredged up from the past by Western orientalists to discredit

Islam. Thus Malik Ghulam Farid claims it 'has been deliberately misinterpreted and its meaning purposely distorted by prejudiced Christian writers . . . the story has been totally rejected as unfounded by all learned commentators of the Qur'an.'[35] Actually, there is no such consensus here: among four leading classical commentators on the Qur'an, only Razi wholly rejects the story of the Satanic Verses. It was accepted by Zamakhshari, probably the greatest of the early Qur'anic commentators,[36] by Al Quturbi[37] and by Al Baidawi[38]; Razi rejected it on the ground that the *isnad* is unsound. 'The story,' says Razi, 'is a fiction invented by apostates and is unfounded.' The historian Ibn Kathir (d. 1373) also regards the *isnad* as unreliable.[39]

Some Muslim scholars, notably Fazlur Rahman, accept the story, as do three leading biographers of the Prophet Muhammad – Sir William Muir, W. Montgomery Watt and Maxime Rodinson. However, at least two modern Western scholars, Count Caetani and John Burton, question its authenticity. Burton, a leading authority on the collection of the Qur'an, argues that the story was invented to illustrate the legal doctrine of 'abrogation', according to which some Qur'anic verses are deemed to be superseded by others as sources of law.[40]

In his novel Rushdie links the incident with other episodes in the accounts of early Muslim annalists which cast doubt on the divinity of the Qur'an: for example, according to a story, also recorded by Tabari, one of the Prophet's scribes, Abdullah ibn Sa'ad, temporarily lost his faith after a mistake he had made in transcription went unnoticed by the Prophet. In Gibreel's dreams the part of Abdullah is given to Salman al Farisi. Salman is an important figure in the early history of Islam. A barber of Persian birth who was adopted into the Prophet's household, he masterminded one of Muhammad's victories over the Meccans by persuading Muhammad to build a defensive ditch around the city of Medina. He is thus 'the symbol of the Persians, who were adopted into Islam, and links the Arabian world with the Iranian tradition'.[41] Much revered by the Shi'a, he is also regarded as one of the founders of Sufism, the mystical tradition in Islam. He is not named as one of Muhammad's scribes. Rushdie's use of this character suggests ironic endorsement of Abdullah's doubt.

The story of the Satanic Verses goes to the heart of the dogma that Muhammad's role in revelation was purely passive, like a 'telephone, a mindless instrument that could in no way interfere with the transmission of the text'.[42] The doctrine was canonised in Sunni Islam from the ninth century CE – at least two centuries after Muhammad's death – in the course of polemics between a group of theologians known as the Mu'tazilis and their opponents, the *ahl al hadith* or 'Hadith Folk'. Reacting against the burgeoning religious and legal authority of the early legal schools, with their 'living' traditions, the Hadith Folk emphasised a style of pietism that recognised no authority outside the divine text and the Prophet's *sunna*. In so doing they initiated a tendency that led towards deification not only of the Prophet, but of the Qur'an, as the 'uncreated' word of God that was a kind of 'eternal cosmic entity, something of God himself'.[43] The Mu'tazilis, who adopted a much more intellectualist approach, saw this as derogating from God's absolute unity; in stressing God's reason they implied that He was bound to reward the good and punish the evil – which caused their opponents, in turn, to accuse them of dishonouring Him, derogating from his absolute sovereignty. During the reign of the Abbasid caliph al Mamun (813–833) the Mu'tazilis gained the ascendancy, and the Hadith Folk were required to undergo a test of orthodoxy, affirming their belief in the doctrine of the 'created' Qur'an. Those who refused to submit, led by Ahmad Ibn Hanbal (780–855), were persecuted. Ibn Hanbal's resistance, which became celebrated as a form of martyrdom, contributed to the discrediting of the Mu'tazilis, and on al Mamun's death the official policy was reversed. Thereafter 'uncreatedness' became part of Sunni orthodoxy. All innovation in law was condemned and the gates of *ijtihad*, of creative interpretation of the divine texts, were firmly closed.

Rushdie's satire, however, goes much further than merely challenging the fundamentalist dogma of an 'uncreated' Qur'an: he casts doubt on the very moral basis of revelation. The themes are elaborated in the passages set in the fabulous city of Jahilia – a kind of Swiftean inversion of Mecca. Jahilia, the city made out of sand, 'the very stuff of inconstancy – the quintessence of unsettlement, shifting, treachery, lack-of-form',[44] bears the same relation to Mecca that Mahound does to Muhammad. In Islamic discourse, the term *jahiliya* refers to the 'period of ignorance' before the coming of Islam. Modern fundamentalists, following Maududi, designate the contemporary Muslim world as *jahiliya*: the word resonates not just with the idea of ignorance, but arrogance and impiety as well. In the theology of doubt, *jahili* is what fundamentalism is: ignorance combined with the arrogance of religious certainty. Jahilia is where Abraham, 'the bastard', abandons his wife Hagar in the waterless wilderness. For the devout Muslim, this act of Abraham, the original *hanif* or monotheist, is a commendable instance of his absolute faith in God; for a modern sensibility, nurtured in a universe where ethics have broken free from the religious matrix, Abraham's act seems appallingly callous: 'From the beginning, men used God to justify the unjustifiable,' comments Rushdie/Gibreel.[45] Baal is the official satirist to the ruler of Jahilia, Abu Simbel, a name which combines Pharaonic overtones with Abu Sufyan, chief of the Qurayshite pagans and Muhammad's leading opponent until his belated acceptance of Islam in 631 AD.

Through the character of the poet Baal, Rushdie infiltrates himself into the narrative of Gibreel's dreams. With characteristic self-mockery, Rushdie undercuts Baal's literary arrogance: his protest that 'it isn't right for the artist to become the servant of the state'[46] is countered by Abu Simbel's observation that many other poets 'make a living by assassination songs'.[47] Baal's dilemma goes to the heart of the religious–literary problematic of Islam. More than any other religion, Islam proclaims itself to be a literary faith. Originating in a pastoral society in which poetry was the most highly prized of the arts, Muhammad's claims to prophethood were vested in speech. He performed no miracles, though after his death miracles were credited to him. Instead he challenged his auditors to produce a single verse of comparable merit to the verses of the Qur'an. The Qur'anic word for verse – *aya* – also means 'miracle' or 'sign'.[48] Some tried, and perhaps succeeded: but inevitably their offerings were dismissed as impious parodies. Since the Qur'an became the absolute standard of literary excellence, its claims were self-validating. The Qur'an is composed in *saj'*, a kind of rhythmic, mnemonic prose which deliberately avoids the more highly wrought style of poetry. Prophet and poets were engaged in intellectual warfare: for the most part the poets articulated the old pagan values which Islam sought to change. 'And as for the poets,' says the Qur'an, '[only] the perverse follow them. Hast thou not seen how they wander in every valley and how they say that which they do not?'[49] Some poets replied with anti-Muslim satires. The most outspoken was a woman, Asma bint Marwan, who taunted and insulted the tribesfolk of Medina for submitting to the Meccan prophet's rule:

> Fucked men of Malik and of Nabit
> And of Awf, fucked men of Khazraj
> You obey a stranger who does not belong among you
> Who is not of Murad, nor of Madhhij
> Do you, when your own chiefs have been murdered, put
>   your hope in him,
> Like men greedy for meal soup when it is coming?
> Is there no man of honour who will take advantage of an
>   unguarded moment,
> And cut off the gull's hopes?[50]

When these and similar verses were reported to the Prophet, he is said to have asked, like Henry II, 'Will no one rid me of this daughter of Marwan?' The same day Umayr ibn Adi, a man from her own clan, went to the poet's house. She was sleeping with her children all around her, the youngest, still a baby, at the breast. Umayr drove his sword through her and returned in triumph. 'You have done a service to Allah and his Messenger,' said the Prophet.[51]

Another pre-Islamic poet, Hassan ibn Thabit, converted to Islam, becoming the Prophet's leading literary apologist. Was his conversion genuine? We cannot be certain. Poets in those days were presumed to possess numinous powers. They put themselves at the disposal of tribal chiefs, writing eulogies for them or satires against their enemies in return for favours. Some of them managed to retain a sceptical temper. One, Shaddad ibn al Aswad al Laythi, is said to have challenged the Prophet's teachings on immortality, and survived.[52] Another early free-thinker, Abu'l Ala al Ma'ari (983–1057 CE), clearly disbelieved in divine revelation. Religion, he thought, was a fable invented by the ancients, worthless except to those who preyed on folly and superstition:

> Hanifs [Muslims] are stumbling, Christians all astray,
> Jews wildered, Magians far on error's way.
> We mortals are composed of two great schools –
> Enlightened knaves or else religious fools.[53]

About ten years before his death at the age of eighty-four the Persian poet Nasr i Khusraw visited Abu'l Ala in his home town in Syria. He described him as the chief man in town, very rich, honoured by the inhabitants and surrounded by more than two hundred students who had travelled far and wide to attend his lectures.[54] The tradition of literary scepticism and literary blasphemy lasted until modern times. As Timothy Brennan has pointed out, even the great Muhammad Iqbal, revered by fundamentalists as the spiritual father of Pakistan, wrote a poem in 1908 in which he accuses God of infidelity. 'At times you have pleased us,' he tells the Almighty, 'at other times (it is not to be said) you are a whore.'[55] In the days before print, telephone, photocopiers and fax machines exposed such irreverent thoughts to the rage of the *jahili* faithful – the orthodoxy of the ignorant – a degree of intellectual freedom existed within the wider framework of Islam, a freedom that, as Rushdie's fate reveals, has become impossible.

Rushdie's disbelieving poet Baal has many Islamic pedigrees. He is, of course, the counterpoise to the austere puritanism represented by the Prophet Mahound, which Rushdie also satirises. The revelation – or recitation – received by Mahound from the dreaming Gibreel tells the faithful how much to eat, how they should sleep, which sexual positions to adopt, the permitted and forbidden subjects of conversations, 'the parts of the body which could not be scratched no matter how unbearably they might itch'. Gibreel vetoes the consumption of prawns and 'requires animals to be killed slowly, by bleeding, so that by experiencing their deaths to the full they might arrive at an understanding of the meaning of their lives for it is only at the moment of death that living creatures understand that life has been real, and not a sort of dream . . .'[56] This last, of course, alludes to the highly sensitive issue of the ritual slaughter of animals for *halal* meat: racists and other critics of Islamic religious practices contend that *halal* killings are cruel, a charge vigorously denied by the Muslims.

What appears to be satirised here is not the Qur'an or even the Prophet's precepts enshrined in the *hadith* literature, but the system of jurisprudence or *fiqh* that derives from them. The jurisconsults or *fuqaha* who constructed the great edifice of Islamic jurisprudence in the early centuries of Islam aimed to achieve a kind of comprehensiveness. Every conceivable human act was classified according to five categories: desirable, permitted, indifferent, disapproved or forbidden. For centuries the *fiqh* remained the essence of Islamic orthopraxis, observance of which was the hallmark of being a Muslim. Most of the actions mentioned in this passage were indeed legislated in some form or other in the compendia of *fiqh*. For example, the *fatawa hindiya*, a sixteenth-century book of *fiqh* widely used in India, rules on such abstruse topics as whether the fast of Ramadan is broken in cases of sex with children.[57] It is not surprising, however, that believing Muslims find it objectionable when such by-products are associated directly with the sacred figure of the Prophet. To retain his sanctity, he must be dissociated from many things that are done in his name. The problem, of course, is that traditionalists who see nothing objectionable in the original structure of *fiqh* continue to use the Prophet to legitimise cruel, repressive or outmoded customs.

A thematic counterweight to the mixing of fact with fantasy in Jahilia, one that testifies to the seriousness of Rushdie's ultimate religious concerns, occurs in the passages describing how Ayesha, the Indian prophetess, leads her followers to drown in the Arabian Sea. For most readers outside the Indian subcontinent the episode (also occurring in one of Gibreel's extended dreams) in which Ayesha persuades her followers to walk across the sea to Mecca would appear as surrealistic fantasy – especially as she is followed everywhere by a cloud of butterflies, a motif suggestive of the 'magic realism' of Borges and Gabriel Garcia Marquez. It is hard for the occidental to believe, even after Jonestown, that such things continue to happen in the real world. Yet the story of Ayesha is based on an actual episode that occurred at Hawkes Bay in Karachi in February 1983, when thirty-eight people, all of them Shi'a, entered the sea in the expectation that a path would open enabling them to walk, via Basra, to the Shi'a holy city of Kerbala in Iraq. The movement was inspired by the leader of the expedition's daughter, Naseem Fatima. For many months Naseem Fatima had been having visions from the Hidden Imam, the Messiah whom the Shi'ites believe will return one day to restore justice and peace to the world. Naseem came from a family of Sayyids (putative descendants of the Prophet Muhammad) in a village in the Jhelum district. Her father, a former air force officer, had made some money working in Saudi Arabia. A shy, withdrawn girl, with a history of fits, she had been unusually devout as a child. The revelations she received began to transform her personality: she became gregarious and confident, gained weight, wore costly dresses and perfumes. She even threw off the veil – a striking gesture for a member of the Sayyid class.

To begin with, she gained quite a few converts who were convinced that the revelations she received were genuine: they included both her parents, a preacher (*zakir*) and a number of lower-class supporters, recent converts to Islam, from a neighbouring village. Not all her relatives, however, believed in her. When she ordered them from 'on high' to redistribute their property, they resisted; while doubts arose when some of the predictions she made about illness, birth or death, failed to come true. A cousin refused her order, transmitted from the Imam, to break off his engagement with a non-Shi'a. She and her father denounced the rebels as *murtids*, apostates, and ordered their relatives to boycott them. Exactly two years after the revelations began, Naseem asked her father a question on behalf of the Hidden Imam: would the faithful plunge into the sea as a witness to their faith? The question was not hypothetical: the believers should walk into the sea, whence they would be miraculously transported to Kerbala in Iraq.

Naseem's father agreed to lead the party, disposing of his

property to pay for the pilgrimage. Forty-two people joined it, ranging in age from eighty years to four months. They travelled to Karachi in trucks, taking with them six massive wooden and tin trunks and Shi'a flags and holy images. The Imam instructed Naseem to place the women and children in the trunks, which were to be locked and pushed into the sea. The remainder would walk. The operation took place at night, and the instructions were obeyed to the letter. One of the trunks was shattered by the waves, but all the remaining occupants were drowned. Most of those who walked into the sea survived: of the eighteen who were drowned, including Naseem Fatima, ten were women, fifteen of them her relatives. Journalists who arrived at the scene with police at dawn reported that the survivors were in high spirits: none showed regret, or remorse, 'only a divine calm, deep ecstasy'.[58] The episode was widely reported and discussed in Pakistan. Reactions were largely determined by sectarian affiliation. The Sunnis generally dismissed the episode as insanity or suicide, a punishable offence in Islam. Shi'a, who resemble some Catholic sects like the Penitentes in their excessive devotion to martyrdom, saw it as a commendable sacrifice that deserved to be rewarded: indeed some wealthy Shi'a immediately produced the money to enable the survivors to travel by air to Kerbala, so that in this respect Naseem's prophecy was fulfilled.

Rushdie incorporates the whole episode into Gibreel's dream narrative, down to its farcical bureaucratic coda – the arrest of the survivors by the Karachi police, who charged them with attempting to leave the country illegally without visas. Interestingly, however, he completely purges it of its sectarian character: in *The Satanic Verses* the Prophetess Ayesha leads her followers towards Mecca, not Kerbala. The significance of this switch is not entirely clear; nor is that of the name Rushdie gives his Prophetess. Fatima – the Prophet Muhammad's daughter, wife of Ali and mother of the martyred Imam Hussein from whom the Twelve Imams of the Shi'a claim descent – is a revered figure in Shi'a Islam: the fact that the Pakistani Sayyid's daughter shared the name of his holy ancestress was a significant element in her cult. Ayesha, the Prophet's youngest and favourite wife, is thoroughly unpopular among Shi'a – not least because she actively opposed the succession of Ali, Fatima's husband, to the leadership of the Islamic community after Muhammad's death. In a sense, the Sunni–Shi'a split in Islam can be traced to the mutual hostility that is said to have existed between Fatima and Ayesha. Was Rushdie trying to tease the Sunnis by associating an episode of Shi'a 'superstitiousness' with the religious mainstream? Was he trying to suggest that religious credulity is not the monopoly of sectarians? Or was he simply indicating in a general sense that the psychic orientation of India's Muslims – not just Shi'a – lies westwards, towards Arabia? 'Islam,' writes Spivak, 'has its head turned away from the subcontinent, across the Arabian Sea.'[59]

By mixing fact and fiction, but in a different way from conventional religion, *The Satanic Verses* makes in its playful and allegorical way a powerful statement about religious doubt, the central condition of modernity. Conveyed in more tactful language the book would doubtless have occasioned some annoyance among Muslim fundamentalists; but it is doubtful if it would have created a national and international uproar.

The focus for the outrage, as both Ali Mazrui and Zaki Badawi testify, is less the raising of doubt than the lampooning of the Prophet. Many Christians, of course, have been similarly offended by the appearance of Christ in profane situations – notably in the recent row over Martin Scorsese's film of Kazantzakis's novel *The Last Temptation*, where Jesus fantasises about sexual relations with Mary Magdalene. To note the parallels, however, is also to become aware of the differences. If *Imitatio Muhammadi*, as Armand Abel has astutely observed, is an imitation of the Prophet's activity, *Imitatio Christi* is rather the imitation of Christ's suffering.[60] Although since the conversion of Constantine Christianity has been associated with secular power, such association goes strongly against the religious grain. To insult Christ is only to offend those Christians who have so lost touch with the Christian *weltanschauung* that they forget that true Christians expect to be insulted, just as Jesus himself was reviled and tormented to death. Christianity thrives on persecution, as witnessed by the current revival of the churches in Eastern Europe. The Christian response to insult is to try to gain the moral and psychological advantage, to 'turn the other cheek'.

The Islamic model is diametrically different. The Prophet did not urge his followers to love their enemies or to turn the other cheek. The Prophet of Islam preached his message during a bloody and violent period in Arabian history. He waged holy war – *jihad* – upon his enemies, the polytheists of Mecca, before overcoming them with superior numbers and force. On occasions he behaved with utter ruthlessness towards his ideological opponents, like his former Jewish allies, the Banu Qurayza, whose males were massacred after the Battle of the Ditch (627 CE). The men – about 600 of them – were all beheaded, apart from those who converted to Islam; the women and children were sold into slavery. Even granted that the Banu Qurayza had betrayed their Muslim allies – a charge they vigorously denied – the sentence nevertheless reveals the gulf between Islamic and Christian values. Plenty of Christians have slaughtered their enemies or imagined enemies in the name of Christ: one has only to recall the notorious remark of the papal envoy Arnald of Cîteaux before the walls of Béziers in southern France, where heretics were protected by Catholics, to be reminded that Islam has no monopoly of militant wrath: 'Kill them all! For God will know his own!' But Christian theology would interpret such cruelty as being the consequence of fallen human nature, not an example of divinely-inspired behaviour to be emulated. The betrayer of Christ was neither avenged by the other disciples, nor tried by any human tribunal: he committed suicide.

This difference has an important bearing on the significance of blasphemy in the two cultures. In Christianity the divine idea is actualised through a body consisting of human beings, the Church. Although Christ founded no church during his lifetime,[61] spiritual power is vested in an institution more or less distinct from the community it purports to serve. In the West blasphemy was assimilated to heresy, an impalpable 'thought crime' whose locus is the human brain. Heresy originated in the Roman law of treason – the ultimate crime against the state. When Christianity became the state cult of the Roman empire, the law of treason was adapted and spiritualised. Heresy became 'treason against God's Majesty' – with a special bureaucracy or 'thought police', namely the Inquisition, charged with determining the limits of ideological acceptability.[62] In due course church and state collaborated in extending legal – and ultimately political – control over human thought and human utterance. The assimilation of blasphemy to heresy coloured subsequent discussion of the issue. For Europeans of the Enlightenment the law of blasphemy was seen as part of the wider apparatus of ecclesiastical repression. Relics of this apparatus remain in Britain, where Christian beliefs are still protected under the blasphemy laws. In June 1976 Mrs Mary Whitehouse of the National Viewers' and Listeners' Association brought a successful prosecution for blasphemous libel against *Gay News* and its editor, Denis Lemon, for publishing James Kirkup's poem 'The Love That Dares To Speak Its Name', an erotic fantasy about the Roman centurion who makes love to the dying Christ after piercing His side on the Cross. The verdict caused an outcry in liberal and literary circles, not least because of the manner in which Judge King Hamilton conducted the trial. Evidence of the poet's intentions was not allowed – indicating that blasphemy was one of the rare crimes where the mental element of intent was absent. The judge's summing-up ignored literary evidence that the poem, like Christ's parables, had to be understood allegorically: 'The words,' he pronounced, 'speak for themselves.' Faced with the defence argument that other controversial works such as Bishop Hugh Montefiore's *Myth of God Incarnate* were equally blasphemous, Judge King Hamilton restated the doctrine first enunciated by Lord Justice Coleridge in 1882: Montefiore's suggestion that Jesus may have been homosexual was not blasphemous because it had been expressed in 'decent language'. His definition of blasphemous libel, however, was restricted to Christianity: 'Blasphemous libel is committed if there is published any writing concerning God or Christ, the Christian religion, the Bible, or some sacred subject, using words which are scurrilous, abusive or offensive and which tend to vilify the Christian religion (and therefore have a tendency to lead to a breach of the peace).'[63]

The *Gay News* case prompted the Law Commission to recommend the complete abolition of the common law offences of blasphemy and blasphemous libel. After taking evidence from 1800 religious organisations and groups it concluded:

1 That the law was discriminatory since blasphemy and blasphemous libel protected only the Christian religion and, it seemed, the tenets of the Church of England.
2 Being offences at common law, not statute offences, there was no agreed definition of the offence, which had been subject to change through court decisions over three centuries.
3 Although a large majority of those who commented on the Law Commission's working paper wanted a law of blasphemy retained, the difficulties of extending the offence to protect other religions were overwhelming.[64]

The Law Commission's recommendations were in line with legal developments in the other major common law country, the United States. Blasphemy and heresy had been on the statute books of several of the American colonies. Despite the disestablishment clause in the First Amendment which demands strict church–state separation, blasphemy laws remain on the statute books of several states.

The US Supreme Court has never ruled directly on the legality of such statutes. Other church–state decisions, however, suggest that they would be unlikely to stand up to the ultimate constitutional test. In 1952 a New York state ban on an allegedly sacrilegious film, *The Miracle*, was unanimously overturned. Justice Tom Clark wrote in Burstyn *v* Wilson, 'It is not the business of government in our nation to suppress real or imagined attacks upon a particular religious doctrine, whether they appear in publication, speeches, or motion pictures.'[65]

With the highest church attendance rates in the industrialised world, American clergy have been much more confident than their British counterparts in their ability to defend religious ideals in open competition. They understood that blasphemy laws, far from defending religious beliefs, tended to undermine them, by hedging them about with the power of the state. As John Adams put it in a letter to his friend Thomas Jefferson, 'I think such laws are a great embarrassment, great obstructions to the improvement of the human mind. Books that cannot bear examination certainly ought not to be established as divine inspiration by penal laws . . . The substance and essence of Christianity, as I understand it, is eternal and unchangeable, and will bear examination forever.'[66]

In Islamic law, the emphasis was always more towards protecting the honour of the Prophet and the Islamic community than regulating religious belief. The most extended treatment of the subject comes in a book by the famous scholar and jurist Ibn Taymiyya.[67] He wrote it to illustrate the legal points arising from his dispute with a Christian cleric accused of insulting the Prophet. Ibn Taymiyya links vilification of the Prophet with disparaging the Muslims: both constitute a *hadd* offence – that is an offence against the 'boundaries' set by God, which cannot be settled by compensation. According to Ibn Taymiyya, anyone defaming the Prophet *must* be executed, whether he is a Muslim or not. There is disagreement among the experts about whether the blasphemer should be allowed to repent. Ibn Taymiyya comes down on the side of those who insist that even if the culprit repents, or converts to Islam in the case of a non-Muslim, he must be killed. Some authorities argued that Jews or Christians who cursed the Prophet should be killed unless they converted to Islam, and there are documented cases where this was applied.

The Islamic laws of blasphemy, of course, only applied in Muslim lands. Classical Jurists divided the world into *Dar al Islam* and *Dar al Harb*, the abode of Islam and the abode of war. *Dar al Islam* is 'liberated' territory where the Law – God's final revelation to humankind – is applied in its entirety. Its rulers, apart from the caliphs, who virtually disappeared from political view after the tenth century CE, are not theocrats: in theory they cannot legislate. The Law having been revealed in its perfection, their duty is to maintain it by 'ordering the good and forbidding the evil'. Subjects are enjoined to obey their rulers, however arbitrary: in a famous phrase quoted with approval by Ibn Taymiyya, 'the Sultan is the Shadow of God on earth. Sixty years with an unjust imam is better than one night of anarchy.'[68]

If the rulers change, or abandon the Law, the territory becomes *Dar al Harb*, the abode of war, like the rest of the world outside *Dar al Islam*. Here, at least in theory, it is incumbent on Muslims to wage the *jihad*, the struggle or Holy War against the unbelievers. The original impulse of Islam, like that of Communism, was global and utopian. The *jihad* would eventually unite the whole world within the abode of Islam (the word, meaning submission or self-surrender to God, has the same root as *salam*, peace). The Divine Law – that essential component of Muslim identity – never wholly reconciled itself to the failure of Islam's original utopian goal of uniting the world under the rule of God. Relations between the two worlds remained theoretically unpeaceful. Assumptions of dominance and subordination continued to prevail. Even commercial relations were discouraged. The Malaki school of law insisted that believers should avoid trading with *Dar al Harb* as much as possible, whether by land or sea.[69] Its founder, Malik ibn Anas (d. 796), says unbelievers may trade with believers and enter *Dar al Islam*, but he discourages believers from visiting *Dar al Harb*. He even suggests that the Caliph should appoint officials at the borders of *Dar al Islam* to prevent believers from leaving.[70] The similarities with the old pre-Gorbachev Soviet bloc are compelling.

It is therefore somewhat ironic that some Muslim activists have tried, so far unsuccessfully, to have *The Satanic Verses* banned under Britain's arcane blasphemy laws, laws that would originally have condemned them as heretics. Under Islamic law, they do not have a leg to stand on: the classical jurists would tell them they were living in *Dar al Harb*. Their duty is not to uphold the honour of Islam in secular infidel courts, but to migrate to a country where the writ of the Divine Law still runs. This peculiar situation has arisen because in this, as in other areas, Britain is irrationally attached to relics of the past. The United States takes a much more robust view of religious outrage. Under the First Amendment, religious freedom and freedom of speech are linked indissolubly: at the same time, no law may be passed pertaining to the establishment of religion. Freedom of speech is the guarantee of freedom of worship. Given the ultimate protection of the law, people are free to question, lampoon, even insult each others' religious beliefs. I myself have attended meetings within a hundred yards of the Temple in Salt Lake City, headquarters of the worldwide Mormon Church, where professional apostates, mostly ex-Mormons, devote their time and energy to fighting what they regard as the lies and falsehoods perpetrated by their Church and its founding prophet, Joseph Smith. Members of the Mormon Church may dislike this activity, but they know that to object would be counter-productive. Muslims in the United States know that nothing they do will cause *The Satanic Verses* to be withdrawn. Their campaign has dwindled accordingly, to the point where a paperback edition of the book appeared almost without protest.

CHAPTER THREE

Islam in Britain

Like Islam in the world at large, Islam in Britain is fragmented into different sects and factions. Since the collapse of the original Arab caliphate, the idea of a single Islamic *umma* or world community of Muslims has been something of a myth – though like all such myths, it retains a powerful hold over the imagination; and since Kemal Ataturk abolished the Ottoman Caliphate in 1924, there has been no institutional leadership in Islam, nothing comparable to a papacy or even a generally recognised congress of mosques on the lines of the conventions of free churches in the Protestant world. Neither in Britain nor anywhere else can any one individual or organisation claim to 'speak for Islam' as the Pope, say, speaks for Catholicism. There are, however, certain institutions that command widespread respect among rank-and-file Muslims, though not among the radicals. One is Al Azhar in Cairo, the world's oldest university, where many of Sunni Islam's leading *ulema* specialists are trained. A *fatwa* by the Sheikh el Azhar carries a good deal of weight – though it is not in any way binding, since on almost any given subject there may be other authorities who will give different rulings. Similarly, in Britain, the Central Mosque and Islamic Cultural Centre at Regent's Park in London, built on land donated to the Muslim community by King George V, has a certain pre-eminence. Its trustees are the ambassadors of all 28 Muslim states. In practice, however, it tends to reflect the views of Saudi Arabia, which pays for the upkeep and salaries of its staff. The Director of the Islamic Cultural Centre – who for many Britons would seem to be the nearest equivalent to the Chief Rabbi or Archbishop of Canterbury – is an accredited Saudi diplomat, not a trained imam.

Elsewhere in Britain, the structure of Islam reflects the heterogeneous ethnicity of the various Muslim communities. The longest established is a community of Yemenites, founded by seamen from Aden who settled in Cardiff before the Second World War. There are also sizeable communities in British cities of Malays (from both Malaysia and South Africa), Turks (from Turkey and Cyprus), Nigerians, Palestinians, Egyptians and other Arabic speakers. By far the majority, however, are immigrants from the Indian subcontinent – Pakistanis, Bangladeshis and Indians – who arrived in Britain in the 1950s and 1960s. These communities include several ethnic and linguistic subgroups: in addition to Urdu and Bengali speakers from the cities and the plains, there is a bewildering variety of peoples from the highlands of the north: Pushtus, Pathans, Punjabis, Mirpuris, Campbellpuris, and Sylhetis all rub shoulders in cities like Bradford, Birmingham and Burnley. As often as not, however, they will worship at different mosques. In addition to these ethnic, territorial and linguistic divisions, the Muslims of subcontinental origins are ranged into a number of different religious tendencies. All of them represent different responses to the crisis experienced by Indian Muslims since the eighteenth century, when British power and the forces of modernity upset the old certainties.

The temper of Indian Islam is, compared with Arab Islam, harsh, neurotic and insecure. Whereas it is incontrovertible that 'God speaks Arabic', the language of the Qur'an, the status of Urdu is much more uncertain. The Qur'an, as an 'uncreated' part of the godhead, cannot be translated; most Muslims in Britain are required to memorise it in Arabic, a language they barely understand. Urdu and English translations were, until quite recently, looked upon askance.

The Mughal conquerors brought India, formally speaking, into *Dar al Islam*. Though they made many converts among the lower Hindu castes, Hinduism proved obstinately resistant to Muhammad's message. Indeed the two religions are diametrically opposed in almost every respect. Whereas Hinduism is a vast, amorphous aggregation of beliefs that evolved in the course of centuries from the sacrificial hymns of the *Vedas* to the philosophical speculation of the *Upanishads* and the discipline of Yoga, Islam is bound by the strict set of rules derived from the Qur'an and the Traditions of the Prophet. Where the temper of Hinduism tends to be 'melancholy, sentimental and philosophical', that of Islam is 'ardent and austere'. Where the Hindu genius flowers in the concrete and iconographic, that of Islam tends to be 'atomistic, abstract, geometrical and iconoclastic'. Despite twelve centuries of settlement and considerable adaptation, Indian Islam retained its largely foreign character. The Indian Muslim remained, in the words of Jadunath Sarkar, 'an intellectual exotic' who felt he was 'in India, but not of it'.[1]

Islam is exclusive: membership of the *umma*, the world-wide Islamic community, sets the believer apart from other forms of group allegiance. Hinduism is inclusive and syncretical: 'the non-proselytising and non-egalitarian resilience of Hinduism' can absorb and assimilate other faiths into its ever-growing, ever-changing spiritual complex, and fitting the former adherents of other faiths into its caste structure. Islam is egalitarian and communal, Hinduism hierarchical and decentralised. Whereas Islam rejects, theoretically at least, a class of specialised interpreters, insisting that all Muslims belong to a single *umma* or nation undifferentiated by wealth or status, the trend of Brahmanical Hinduism has been to accept all worship and to reject none, to bridge the gap between popular fetishism and learned Vedantism, to ensure that the superstitious cults of the illiterate masses remain in at least oblique touch with the metaphysical speculation of the higher intellectual order, and thus to crystallise an ascending hierarchy of religious faith corresponding to the socio-economic scale of caste-structure.' Whereas Muslim interpreters of the Qur'an and the Traditions are bound by the weight of scholarly consensus to follow the 'straight path' of truth, Hinduism is ever open to new ideas. It can even, if necessary, find room for new gods. Every passage in the Hindu sacred texts is open to figurative interpretation, so that it is possible for different schools of Hinduism 'to hold diametrically opposed doctrines without serious antagonism'.[2] For the Muslim, Hinduism represents polytheism, *the* original religious sin in Islam, in its most palpable, exuberant and offensive form. The very existence of Hinduism is an affront to the Muslim sensibility, a perpetual, living challenge to the revealed truths Muslims hold dear.

Indian Islam was not always intransigent: the Mughal emperor Akbar (1556–1605) made a serious effort to create an ecumenical state by placing his Hindu subjects on a level of equality with the Muslims. Proclaiming himself a *mujtahid* – an independent interpreter of the law – he changed those aspects of the Shari'a which emphasised Hindu inferiority, including the poll tax and the rules governing intermarriage. In 1581 he promulgated the 'Divine Faith' (*Din Illahi*), a version of higher Sufism which he hoped would provide a common basis for Muslim and Hindu worship. The experiment, however, was a failure: deprived of their distinctive identity and sense of historical mission as bearers of God's final message to humankind, the Muslims turned against Akbar's ideas. The reaction was spearheaded by the orthodox Naqshbandi order under Sheikh Ahmed Sirhindi in the seventeenth century and Shah Wali Ullah in the eighteenth. Although syncretism continued at a popular level among the Sufi *tariqas* or brotherhoods, no more efforts were made to create a common ideology from the top.

The coming of the British in India led to an agonised debate about whether India should be considered *Dar al Islam* or *Dar al Harb*. Some authorities argued that since the land was no longer under Islamic government, it should be treated as *Dar al Harb*. Thus in 1803 Shah Abdul Aziz, the son of Shah Wali Allah, pointed out that in the city of Delhi 'The Imam of the Muslims wields no authority at all, whereas the authority of the leaders of the Christians is enforced – without any trouble. By the enforcement of the rules of unbelief is meant that unbelievers can act on their own authority in governing and dealing with the subjects, in collecting land-tax, tolls, tithes, customs and excises, in punishing highway robbers and thieves, settling disputes and in punishing crimes' – in other words, in performing the traditional functions of the Muslim Sultan or Amir.[3]

The logical inference to be drawn from this ruling was that the faithful should declare the *jihad* against the British, if necessary after making the *hijra* or emigration to part of *Dar al Islam*. This was in fact the course taken by Sayyid Ahmed Barelwi

(1786–1831), with the support of the prestigious Shah Wali Ullah family. Barelwi began by starting a rigidly puritanical movement, the Tariqa-i-Muhammadi (Path of Muhammad) that adhered to strict monotheistic principles, inveighing against religious innovations and all forms of polytheism. Having acquired a considerable following among peasants and craftsmen in Bengal and northern India who had suffered economically under British rule, Sayyid Ahmed went on to prepare for a *jihad* against the infidels. In 1826, following the Prophet's example, he migrated from the *Dar al Harb* of India to the nearest available portion of *Dar al Islam*, the North-West Frontier, near the Afghan border. Here he hoped to found an Islamic state on liberated territory. The Sikhs, however, stood in his way, and Barelwi was killed by them in 1831. His successors continued the struggle from Sittana on the North-West Frontier for half a century until they were finally suppressed by the British in 1883. Members of the Tariqa-i-Muhammadi played an active part in the Mutiny in 1857. In several places during the rising *fatwas* were issued declaring the rising a *jihad* (although Hindus, of course, played an active part alongside the Muslims).

The failure of the Mutiny convinced members of the Muslim middle classes that resistance to the British was pointless, and that their interests would be better served by loyalty to the British Empire. From around 1870 *fatwas* began to appear stating that Indian Muslims were not obliged by their religion to fight against the British. Thus the *ulama* of northern India, while arguing that India was still *Dar al Harb*, stated that this did not entail *jihad* because the Muslims were *protected* by the Christians. The Muhammadan Literary Society of Calcutta went much further in the direction of collaboration by declaring that India was *Dar al Islam*, and that *jihad* was therefore forbidden: 'If anyone were to wage war against the Ruling Powers of this Country, British India, such a war would be rightly pronounced rebellion; and rebellion is strictly forbidden by the Muhammadan Law.' The position that *jihad* was unlawful was argued systematically by Sayyid Ahmed Khan (1817–98), the foremost modernist thinker in nineteenth-century India and founder of the famous Muhammadan Anglo-Oriental College at Aligarh. According to Ahmed Khan, *jihad* was only lawful in the case of positive oppression or obstruction of Muslims in the exercise of their religious duties – namely the 'five pillars' consisting of the declaration of faith, prayer, fasting, tithing (*zakat*) and pilgrimage. The position of India as *Dar al Harb* or *Dar al Islam* could be argued either way: it would be better to call it *Dar al Aman*, the 'land of security':

> It will thus be seen, that an Infidel Government in which the Mahomedans enjoy every sort of peace and security, discharge their religious duties with perfect freedom, and which is connected with a Mahomedan Government by a treaty, is not Dar al Islam, because it is a Non-Mahomedan Government, but we may call it so as regards the peace and religious freedom which the Moslems enjoy under its protection; nor is it Dar al Harb, because the treaty existing – between it and the Moslem Government makes Jihad against it unlawful . . . The proper term would . . . rather be Dar al Aman, or 'land of security' in which the Muslim may lawfully reside as a mustamin, or seeker of aman.[4]

Sayyid Ahmed Khan became a keen Anglophile; he adopted Western dress and visited England, where he attended Charles Dickens's last public reading, and met Thomas Carlyle. British rule in India, he told the Viceroy, Lord Lytton, was 'the most wonderful phenomenon the world has ever seen', loyalty to which sprang 'not from servile submission to foreign rule, but from genuine appreciation of the blessings of good government'. In 1887, the year he advised his fellow-Muslims not to join the National Congress, he was appointed to the Viceregal Legislative Council. He was knighted the following year. He was the first of many Muslim intellectuals for whom the path of modernism led to accommodation and ultimately collaboration with colonialism. And, like so many others, he left his people behind.

The Islam of the people remained divided into two broad tendencies: the Islam of the villages, where the mystical practices of Sufism allowed a good number of Hindu beliefs to undermine the strictness of Islam; and the more rigid Islam of the cities, where reformers or *mujaddids* strove to purge Islam of such innovations or accretions, including the cults of saints and holy men.

The largest of the original rural-based groups consisted of the Barelwis. Ahmad Riza Khan Barelwi (1856–1929) was a traditionalist who sought to preserve the popular devotional characteristics of Indian Islam, especially as practised in rural areas, with its admixture of Sufi mysticism, focused on the cult of the saints, who were presumed to have wide intercessionary powers. Chief among these holy figures was the Prophet himself. Ahmad Riza adhered to the gnostic concept of the Divine Light of Muhammad which filtered down to the holy men or *pirs*, both living and dead, who abounded in India. As possessors of a portion of the Divine Light their intercessions could be called upon, not just at their shrines, but everywhere. The Barelwis pay special attention to the *Mawlid al Nabi* or Prophet's birthday, which they honour by a period of ritual 'standing', during which the Prophet's spirit is supposed to be among them. They also celebrate the death-days of several Muslim saints, including Abdul Qadir Gilani, a revered figure of early Islam and the supposed founder of the Sufi *tariqa* to which Ahmad Riza belonged.[5]

Ahmad Riza's core of supporters were Pathans from the major cities around Bareilly in Uttar Pradesh and the Punjab, but as his movement grew and became more self-conscious it gained general support among rural Muslims and illiterates with no direct access to the scriptures. A man of considerable wealth as well as vast learning, especially in the Hanafi school of law, Ahmad Riza dispensed largesse to his followers in the manner of a religious prince. In politics he was generally pro-British: he supported the Empire during the First World War and organised the traditionalist *ulema* against the movement, backed by Gandhi and the Congress Party, which protested against the abolition of the Ottoman Caliphate in 1924 – an act deemed to have been engineered by the British to undermine Islam.

At the other end of the Indo-Muslim religious spectrum, also well represented in Britain, lie the reformists or Deobandis, named after their principal seminary at Deoband about ninety miles north-east of Delhi. Like other Islamic reformers in Arabia and North Africa, the Deobandis believed that the only way Muslims could effectively challenge Christian or Western hegemony was by returning to the purity of the Qur'an and the Prophet's *sunna*, purged of all the accretions that had built up around them during the centuries. They believed that only by recovering the pristine Islam of the Prophet and his Companions would the Muslims ever regain their former greatness. In contrast to the Barelwis, they avoid extravagant customs like lavish weddings and dowries. They utterly reject the concept of saintly intervention, either in this world or the next. Instead they foster observance of the Law by inculcating a sense of personal responsibility. In addition to active proselytising, they publish reformist tracts on moral and social behaviour. They explicitly try to include women in their evangelical enterprise, emphasising that the quintessentially feminine virtues of modesty and deference should apply to masculine conduct as well.[6]

Deobandis lay particular stress on Qur'anic study and law. They have built *madrasas* or Islamic seminaries all over India, and their headquarters at Deoband is regarded by many people as the foremost centre of Islamic learning after Al Azhar in Egypt. They have translated classical texts from Arabic and Persian into Urdu and other Indian languages. Under the Raj they tried to ensure that the Muslims should have as little as possible to do with the British-run *kafir* state. Having created systems operating outside the state, their idea of independence ultimately consisted in the rule of the *ulema*. Like other *ulema*, they opposed the idea of Pakistan once they realised that it would be ruled by secular-minded Muslims. They thought they would have a better chance of exercising power within a secular India, where they hoped – quite unrealistically – to be granted judicial autonomy.

A more radical version of the same reformist, puritanical tendency exists in the Ahl-i-Hadith. Unlike the Deobandis, who accepted the core doctrines of the four legal schools of Sunni Islam, the Ahl-i-Hadith rejected the medieval legacy of law altogether, making use only of the Qur'an and *hadith*. The style of the Ahl-i-Hadith is similar to that of its predecessors of the same name under the Abbasid Caliphate: it is iconoclastic and

narrow. Like the Saudi Arabians, who officially adhere to Wah-
habi tenets, they strictly forbid anything resembling 'saint-
worship', including worship at the tombs of the Prophet and
his family. The Ahl-i-Hadith make a habit of saying 'amen'
aloud in their prayers in addition to other differences in ritual
which other Sunni Muslims find offensive. In the nineteenth
century there were riots after the ordinary Hanafis tried to ban
them from their mosques.

Another offshoot of the reformist tradition of Deoband is the
influential missionary organisation Jamaat Tabligh ul Islam (also
known as Tablighi Jamaat) which was founded by an alumnus
of Deoband, Maulana Muhammad Ilyas (1885–1944). It is particularly active among Muslim immigrants in Europe. Ilyas,
who preached among poor, uneducated, socially marginal Meos
in the rural Mewat region south-west of Delhi, is in some ways
comparable to John Wesley in Britain. Like Wesley, he injected
an element of inner piety into the reformist tradition which
made it highly adaptable to the experience of the displaced
migrant, whether from countryside to city or from one continent
to another. He taught that Muslims must no longer be content
with the outward observance of law and ritual, but should
actively promote Islam by 'enjoining the good and forbidding
the evil' in a spirit of brotherly love. Above all they must seek
to convert by persuasion, abandoning any idea of imposing
Islam by political means. Members are forbidden to discuss
politics while preaching, or to engage in religious controversy
with other Muslims. For Tablighis, observance of the Shari'a
law, as set out in the medieval textbooks, is essentially a personal matter. Male members of the Tablighi Jamaat prefer to
wear beards – traditional marks of Muslim piety. On Fridays,
at least, and other ceremonial occasions, they also wear the red
or white Muslim cap and the traditional kurta-pyjama, with
white baggy trousers and waistcoats. Their appeal is primarily
to the least educated, which partly accounts for their success
among immigrants in Western Europe. They are said to be
recipients of generous amounts of Saudi Arabian money.[7]

Among the better educated, two Islamic movements, both
originating in India, exercise an influence out of proportion to
their numbers. The Ahmadiyya is a heterodox messianic sect

that proselytises widely in the West. It developed during the nineteenth century as a direct response to Hindu revivalism and Christian missionary activity under the British Raj. Its founder, Mirza Ghulam Ahmad (1839–1908) of Qadian in the Eastern Punjab, began his career as a champion of Islamic orthodoxy. In 1891, however, he proclaimed himself the Messiah or Mahdi; in due course he announced he was receiving revelations directly from God. Like Akbar's Din Illahi, there was a strong element of syncretism in his outlook: he proclaimed himself to be both an avatar of Krishna and the *buruz* (reappearance) of Muhammad. Among his more bizarre doctrines was his claim that Jesus recovered after 'swooning' on the Cross, that he travelled to Kashmir and Afghanistan in order to convert the Ten Lost Tribes of Israel residing there, and that he drank and consorted with prostitutes, before dying in Sringar, Kashmir, where he is buried.

The Ahmadis' heterodox views caused them to be attacked, sometimes violently, by other Muslims. In 1953 there were serious disturbances in Pakistan resulting from demands by conservative Muslims that the Ahmadiyya should be declared a non-Muslim sect. Although the secular-minded government refused to give way, the demand was revived in the 1970s when, under renewed fundamentalist pressure, the government of Zulfikar Ali Bhutto excluded the Ahmadis from holding public office. Since then the Ahmadiyya have moved their world headquarters to Wimbledon in London.[8]

The leading figure in the anti-Ahmadiyya agitation in Pakistan in 1953 was the fundamentalist leader and intellectual, Maulana Abu'l Ala Maududi (1903–79), the founder of the extreme right-wing Jamaat-i-Islami. In marked contrast to the Jamaat-i-Tabligh, the Jamaat-i-Islami aims to bring about a full-blooded 'restoration' of Islamic government by the direct exercise of political power. It has close links with the Muslim Brotherhood in Egypt and its affiliates in the Arab world, which share its ambitions. Indeed, Maududi had a powerful influence on the thinking of one of the Brotherhood's leading intellectuals, Sayyid Qutb, executed by Gamal Abdul Nasser in 1960. Moreover, despite differences in theology, there are close affinities between Maududism and the Shi'a Islamic fundamen-

talism of Ayatollah Khomeini which was swept into power by
the Iranian revolution of 1979.

Maududi is probably the most systematic of the modern
Islamic thinkers. Whereas the 'Islamism' of other fundamentalists, including Khomeini, contains a somewhat *ad hoc* mixture
of ingredients, including nationalism, xenophobia and unre-
flective traditionalism, Maududi recognised that in order to
resist Western cultural encroachments Islam had to be reformu-
lated into a full-blooded political ideology. For Maududi and
his followers Islam is entirely self-sufficient and does not need to
explain itself in terms other than its own. The basic proposition,
from which all else flows, is the sovereignty of God: men are
commanded to obey the law of God as revealed in the Qur'an
and the *Sunna*. There is no question of cultural relativism here,
no suggestion that what Maududi is advocating is confined to
the Islamic world:

> The Qur'an does not claim that Islam is the true compendium
> of rites and rituals, and metaphysical beliefs and concepts,
> or that it is the proper form of religious (as the word religion
> is nowadays understood in Western terminology) attitude of
> thought and action for the individual. Nor does it say that
> Islam is the true way of life for the people of Arabia, or
> for the people of any particular country or for the people
> preceding any particular age (say the Industrial Revolution).
> No! Very explicitly, for the entire human race, there is only
> one way of life which is Right in the eyes of God and that is
> `al-Islam.[9]

According to Maududi, all that is required for the just society
is that the righteous should hold political power: for 'societies
are built, structured and controlled from the top down by the
conscious manipulation of those in power'. Human society,
according to Maududi,

> is like a carriage. Just as a carriage goes where the driver
> wishes, so a human society goes where the leaders desire. It
> is obvious that common people must act according to the
> pattern ordained by those who possess power, who control

the means of forming public opinion, who form the systems for individual and social life, who determine the standards of morality etc. If these are in the hands of righteous people, worshippers of God, then it is inevitable that the whole of social life will be God-worshipping . . . None of the purposes of religion can be accomplished so long as control of affairs is in the hands of *kafirs*.[10]

Strongly influenced by the political climate of the 1930s, Maududi cited Italian Fascists, German Nazis and Russian Communists as examples of small, informed and dedicated groups capable of seizing power and exercising it effectively. While disagreeing with their ideologies, he admired their methods. In the case of Islam, he believed, there was no danger of totalitarianism: God's commands carried out by a virtuous elite could not be other than benevolent and just.[11]

Unlike the traditionalist *ulema*, including the Deobandis, who considered themselves bound by precedent in interpreting Islamic law, Maududi accepted the principle of *ijtihad* or the use of independent reasoning in interpreting the law, a view he shared with modernists like Sayyid Ahmad Khan. His conclusions, however, were the opposite of modernist. For instance, he believed in the strictest form of purdah for women, and condemned birth control, arguing that pressure of population leads to the desirable goal of economic development.[12]

The Maududists were enthusiastic supporters of General Zia ul Haqq's Islamisation policies in Pakistan during its initial phase in the early 1970s. Later, as Zia became more isolated, they opportunistically withdrew their support and even joined with the opposition parties in calling for the restoration of democracy – despite Maududi's claim that multi-party democracy was contrary to Islam.

Salman Rushdie, as one would expect, had little time for the Maududists: in one of the interpolations which occasionally interrupt the narrative of *Shame*, Rushdie makes his attitude quite explicit:

So-called Islamic 'fundamentalism' does not spring, in Pakistan, from the people. It is imposed on them from above.

Autocratic regimes find it useful to espouse the rhetoric of faith, because the people respect that language, are reluctant to oppose it. This is how religions shore up dictators; by encircling them with words of power, words which the people are reluctant to see discredited, disenfranchised, mocked.

In the same passage, Rushdie explicitly refers to the Jamaat-i-Islami. While acknowledging that the Jamaat enjoyed some support among college students, Rushdie points out that relatively few people have ever voted for it in an election – a judgement fully vindicated in the 1988 election which brought Benazir Bhutto to power, when the Jamaat were practically eliminated.

Despite their poor showing at the polls, the Jamaatis in Pakistan are generally disciplined and well educated. They publish large quantities of propaganda based on the writings of Maududi and his followers, such as the Jamaat's vice-chairman Khurshid Ahmad, an economics professor and former minister of planning in the Pakistan government. The Jamaat's considerable influence in Britain is thought to be due to the access it has to Saudi funds through the World Islamic League, a pan-Islamic organisation based in Mecca. In the nature of things, however, the extent of this funding is difficult to determine. During a visit to the United Kingdom in 1987 King Fahad of Saudi Arabia is believed to have disbursed some four million pounds in charitable gifts to Muslim organisations, most of which are thought to have had a Jamaati or Deobandi orientation. The Jamaat's main evangelical organisation in Britain is the UK Islamic Mission. Based in London, it has branches in most British cities where there are large Muslim populations, including Manchester, Oldham, Rochdale, Liverpool, Blackpool, Blackburn, Walsall, Birmingham, Wolverhampton and Southampton. Its centre for propaganda is the Islamic Foundation in Leicester. Through the Saudi connection, it exercises a considerable influence on the Islamic Cultural Centre in London.

Before the Rushdie Affair produced a closing of ranks among Muslims in Britain, little love was lost between the different Islamic sects. The Barelwis resented the access the more orthodox Deobandis and Maududists had to Arab funding. The

Maududists in particular have been able to acquire Saudi funds, largely because of the extent to which the narrow and puritanical version of Islam corresponds with the strict fundamentalist tendency current in Saudi Arabia, based on the teachings of Ibn Hanbal and his eighteenth-century disciple Muhammad ibn Abdul Wahhab.

In 1985 the Barelwis held a major conference in London to protest against the mistreatment of Barelwi pilgrims visiting the Holy Places in Saudi Arabia. About 3,000 delegates, bussed from cities all over Britain, passed resolutions condemning the Saudi authorities for preventing pilgrims from worshipping at the tombs of the Prophet and his family in Medina, and for burning copies of Ahmad Riza's Urdu translation and commentary on the Qur'an: this they regarded as a serious act of blasphemy or desecration, since like all Muslim translations, the Barelwi Qur'an includes 'God's speech' in the original Arabic text.

Other disputes have had a more local character: a typical example occurred in Manchester in 1985 over the 'Id al Fitr at the end of the Ramadan fast. Rival Muslim factions quarrelled over the timing of the festival, which begins with the sighting of the new moon. Some of them dated the feast from the sighting of the moon in Saudi Arabia, others in Egypt. Too much was at stake to rely on the ocular test in Britain's cloudy skies. Various attempts have been made to create a single Muslim organisation to settle such disputes. So far, no one organisation commands universal support.

Many of the disputes occurring in British mosques have political origins. In London's Whitechapel district, for example, ordinary Bengali Muslims were outraged when their brand-new mosque, built partly with Saudi money, but also out of contributions from the faithful, was placed in the charge of a board of trustees whose members included the ambassadors of Saudi Arabia and Pakistan but not that of Bangladesh, the country where the great majority of worshippers at this particular mosque originated. The appointment of Mr Moinuddin Chowdery as chairman was regarded as particularly objectionable by most of the Bengadeshis, as he had fought on the Pakistani side during the War of Independence. After pressure from the congregation, Mr Chowdery was forced to resign as chairman, though he remained on the board. Not the least of the ironies flowing from the anti-Rushdie agitation has been the consolidation of right-wing control, including that of the Jamaatis, over mosques and other Islamic institutions that had previously been open to more liberal elements. *The Satanic Verses* provided the Maududists and other hard-liners the opportunity to increase their influence, vindicating their thesis that no compromise was possible between the absolute truths of Islam and the falsehoods of the infidel, *jahili* West.

For a northern British industrial town Bradford is unusually attractive. Its centre, consisting of dull modernist shopping precincts surrounded by a network of ring roads, is rather nondescript, like so many cities that fell victim to post-war planners: apart from the restored Alhambra theatre and one or two fine Victorian municipal buildings, there is nothing to catch the eye. But the city's setting in a valley surrounded by hills is superb. The rows of stone-built back-to-back dwellings, with the gardens situated in front, snake away from the centre along the hillsides, gradually merging with outer townships like Heaton, Keighley or Bingley. An industrial landscape, it is nevertheless built to a human scale: the mills and factories, constructed in stone, seem benign rather than satanic. Even the mill-owners' mansions which now serve the city as pubs or hotels, pretentious villas with towers and castellations set in comfortable grounds, seem more quaint than oppressive. That hated mythological figure, the Victorian capitalist, lived much closer to his workforce than his anonymous descendant, the corporate executive.

The first Indo-Pakistani settlers to arrive in Bradford were former seamen who found themselves stranded during the Second World War in ports like Liverpool and Hull and were directed to work in the munitions factories. Their economic success encouraged others to follow; after the war they began working in the textile and engineering industries. Almost all were single men from a surprisingly small number of localities: Mirpur in Azad Kashmir, the Chhachh district of Campbellpur (now re-named Attock) near the North-West Frontier – 'a corner of the world so obscure,' as Dervla Murphy points out, 'that it doesn't show up even in the *Times Atlas*';[13] Jhelum, Lyallpur, Rawalpindi and other neighbouring districts of West Punjab; the Pathan tribal areas of Mardan, Peshawar and Swat on the North-West Frontier; and the Sylhet district of what is now Bangladesh.[14] Most of them came from families of small land-holders and sharecroppers who lived at a level little above subsistence. Dervla Murphy, who visited Campbellpur in the summer of 1963, found it desperately poor and blisteringly hot:

> There are few trees, little greenery: on every side stretch bare stubble fields and arid wastes of rock and stony soil. One of the most appalling local sights is a cow in calf: so underfed you can plainly see the whole shape of the calf in the womb. Most humans also look underfed . . . Eighty per cent of the girls still marry as soon as they reach puberty and produce ten, twelve, quite often fifteen children, seventy per cent of whom are born diseased – but fated to live on as semi-invalids because epidemics are coming under control.[15]

The Campbellpuris, Mirpuris and other rural Pakistani men came to Britain to earn the extra cash required to raise the family's status back home by increasing its stock or landhold-ings. As there was no primogeniture in Pakistan, every man regarded it as his duty to accumulate as much land as possible to provide for his children.

At first there were very few women: each migrant planned to return home after a few years, to be replaced by another member of the family who would maintain the flow of remit-tances. The Campbellpuris, for example, had a tradition, going back to the turn of the century, of working as stokers in the Merchant Navy, and it was not difficult for the pioneer settlers in Bradford to arrange for their kinsmen to be recruited as seamen in the hope of finding their way to Britain. Other families had to raise the cash for the fare and passport – a very substantial investment costing between ten and thirty times the average *per capita* income, which in Pakistan stood at about £30 per year. The sponsorship system which grew up ensured a steady flow of migrants, to the mutual advantage of the British and local economies. However, around 1960 it became clear that new immigration controls would restrict the movement of men and prevent children from entering Britain unless both parents were already resident.

During the 'beat the ban' period before the 1962 Immigration Act became law, thousands of women and children arrived to join their menfolk. Legislation designed to keep out the immigrants had the effect of converting temporary into permanent settlement. At the same time the localised character of the migrants' places of origin enabled them to maintain the tight kinship structure of their home villages, ensuring that cultural adaptation was kept to the minimum. In effect, they were not so much immigrants as transplants, representing a kind of Raj in reverse: just as the British officers, civil servants and their memsahibs managed to preserve in India the values and customs of Surrey and Berkshire, so Mirpuris, Campbellpuris and Sylhetis preserved in Bradford and other British cities the values and customs of their villages – a world almost as distant culturally from the great Islamic cosmopolitan centres like Cairo or Baghdad as it was from Britain itself.

For the mature generation, transplantation could be effected without serious trauma, at least in declining industrial cities like Bradford. In quarters like the Manningham district the back-to-back cottages were relatively cheap (about £80 or so in the early 1960s) and could be obtained, without loans, for a deposit of £10 or £12, plus weekly instalments of 15s (75p) or £1. As the migrants became established in their adopted city, proportionally less money was sent back to Pakistan, with more being invested in Bradford. Pakistani landlords rented rooms to new immigrants; Pakistani entrepreneurs invested part of their wages saved from working the mills and factories in corner shops and cafés, newsagents, *halal* butcheries, groceries, pharmacies, boutiques, clubs, restaurants, cinemas, laundromats, bookshops, driving schools, travel agencies and a host of other goods and services. Broadly speaking, the same pattern applied to other cities in the North and Midlands and parts of London, such as Southall and Stepney.

Although a certain proportion of Bradford Muslims were employed in the public services such as transport, their connection with the state was minimal. Aspiring to self-sufficiency, caring dutifully for their old as well as their young, the Asians had, according to a Bradford Council report 'a vastly lower social services referral rate' than whites and 'significantly under-used most services'.[16] At times of economic recession they have relied on their own networks of self-help and patronage to find new jobs or sources of income. Those who drew social security benefits in the early 1970s, according to Badr Dahya, saved as much as half for remittances to Pakistan. It is the community support system, rather than the state, which shelters the immigrant from the winds of economic hardship:

> During the period of his unemployment (and sickness), the immigrant-tenant is charged no rent by the immigrant landlord and may be asked to contribute only a token sum, if at all, to his weekly grocery bill, and mutual aid within the immigrant house sees to his other needs. Further, when an unemployed immigrant happens to have his wife and children with him in this country, he does not, like his native counterpart, have 'council house' rents to pay nor, like him, does he have to meet weekly instalments for, say, dining-room or bedroom suites, vacuum cleaner, and so on.[17]

Though many Asians have come to be Labour supporters, this is less a reflection of socialist preferences than a response to the perceived racism of Conservative politicians. If race were taken out of the equation, many, perhaps most, Bradford Muslims, would reveal themselves to be model Tory citizens.

At the heart of community life stands the network of mosques. The Muslims created mosques by knocking terraced houses together, making large upper rooms, and eventually acquired sites where 'proper' mosques, with domes and minarets, could be built. They preferred to make them within walking distance of their places of work, so that the five times daily prayer could be performed in the mosque, not just the noon prayer on Fridays: *salaat* is a communal, physical act, like gym or PT: by performing it with others the individual not only turns his thoughts to God – he merges his individuality with the group, reinforcing his sense of group identity. The mosque, moreover, is not just a place of worship. It is a social and cultural centre, a club where the Muslim meets his fellows, exchanges news and gossip, makes business contacts and strikes deals.

The *imam* of the mosque has no priestly office or pastoral role: he is merely a leader of prayer with a knowledge of the scriptures and the Law. The Muslims of Bradford, like the Muslims in Britain generally, import their *imams* direct from Pakistan, often from their home villages. This reinforces the ties with the homeland, creating an anchor with the certainties of the past. It also reinforces isolation: few of the *imams* know English; fewer still are aware of the wider British society around them with its complexities and diversified spiritual resources. The leaders add spiritual authority to a vision of society already viewed, one might say distorted, through the prism of faith: the society that corresponds to the *jahiliya* of the Prophet's time, a godless, materialistic society wholly dedicated to the pursuit of worldly wealth and sensual pleasure.

This vision is reinforced by what the Muslim leaders choose to see in the surrounding white culture: Western society is portrayed as 'meaningless, aimless, rootless, characterised by vandalism, crime, juvenile delinquency, the collapse of marriages and psychic disorders'.[18] The more positive aspects of Western society – the vigour of its culture in music, art and literature, in film and theatre – elude him utterly, while its greatest virtues – its perilous questioning of its own assumptions, its rejection of dogmatisms, the fact that doubt and scepticism are central to its intellectual outlook, enabling new sciences and new technologies to take root – are turned against it. Such problems as alcoholism, drug and child abuse, discussed in Western newspapers, are by definition 'Western' diseases, unknown to Islam. This attitude of moral superiority towards everything Western compensates psychologically for the experience of powerlessness: but it also reinforces Muslim isolation, the sense of being a people apart in a hostile world.

It would be wrong, of course, to identify such parochialism as inherently 'Islamic', any more than the narrow philistinism of some Irish priests is typically Catholic. While traditional Islamic education tends to foster an idealised vision of the past and an unquestioning belief in the Qur'an as a revealed text, the text itself is full of appeals to reason and knowledge. It was by following their Prophet's injunctions to learn from the more advanced cultures surrounding them that the conquering Arabs became masters not only of the geography of the Fertile Crescent, but its artistic and intellectual heritage as well. The insular character of Islam in Britain has more local explanations: its embattled origins in India, where the threat of Hindu engulfment and communal strife endowed the Islamic outlook with a paranoid streak; and the culture of the village, with its oscillating polarities of honour and shame.

Izzat is the concept of honour widely applied in rural Pakistan. It serves the extended family's identity, endowing it with continuity and value. Since it is held most strongly among groups like the Pathans which still retain a tribal structure, it seems probable that it originated in inter-tribal strife and competition.[19] It is not dissimilar to the concept of *muruwah* as practised among the pagan tribes of Arabia during Muhammad's time. Islam reoriented this concept within the monotheistic framework, so that the honour that was previously vested in the tribe applied to the whole Muslim community or *Umma* in its relations with the world at large. *Izzat* as such is not necessarily 'Islamic': equivalent customs based around honour and shame are found in many other societies – for example, in Greece and Sicily. But it is a component element in Muslim identity, especially in rural or nomadic societies.

A family's *izzat* is vested in its women. What Gilsenan writes of the Levant is true of many other Islamic societies, notably the rural communities in the Indian subcontinent:

In a society such as north Lebanon both *batin* [the hidden realm known only to God and religious leaders endowed with gnostic insight] and sexuality are in the realm of power and the conceptions of power in the symbolic and social systems. Who marries whom, who has sexual relations with whom, the constraints on both and the choices involved are major issues for group structure and relations. Moreover infringement of the rules of conduct, of the ideologically dominant code of honour and shame, the pollution of individuals and family name by female sexuality outside the bounds of marriage, pose a terrible threat to the whole conception of the meaning of relations between male and female worlds and among males. Honour and shame, purity and pollution are vital concerns of life.[20]

In a rural milieu where women live within the extended family, or those male relatives who are forbidden to them sexually under Islamic law, *izzat* is not usually endangered. As a girl from the Jhelum area explained to Amrit Wilson, in the village all the men are 'our *biradiri* (brethren). So women do not need to wear *burkhas* (the complete veil worn by women in Afghanistan and the subcontinent) to avoid being seen by strange men. But in towns, even in small towns, it is not the same. People from different families live and work in the same area and as a result women are forced into *burkhas*.'[21] Conditions in Britain pose a constant threat to a family's *izzat*. At least twenty per cent of Muslim women go out to work, bringing them into contact with strangers; both men and women are subject to racial hostility. In general, says Amrit Wilson, the disregard in British society for 'family and group identity provide an atmosphere in which *izzat* is constantly at risk and therefore is constantly charged and recharged'.

Izzat is the submergence of the individual's identity within the group – or rather, as Dervla Murphy puts it, 'the prevention by the group of the emergence of individuality'.[22] It is mostly women who pay the price. *Izzat* effectively sanctions the sexual double standard which, while not being necessarily Qur'anic, can find a Qur'anic rationale in polygyny (the fact that one man can have up to four wives and not *vice versa*), legal discrimination against women as witnesses and in inheritance, the sanctioning of slavery (and hence concubinage) and other male supremacist assumptions. *Izzat* is not placed in jeopardy by a man who rapes the wife who hates him four times each night; it is by a daughter who rebels against an arranged marriage and elopes with a boy of her choice. *Izzat* is not threatened by men who drink, gamble, consort with prostitutes;[23] but it is placed in mortal peril by a teenage girl who so much as meets with a boy merely to *talk* in the school playground.[24] It is to protect *izzat* that some families withdraw their girls from school at puberty, or refuse to allow girls who have been offered university places to take them up.

Izzat, in the wider sense of the honour of the Muslims as a group *vis-à-vis* white society, was at the root of the Honeyford affair – a controversy which revealed many of the attitudes that would surface even more passionately during the anti-Rushdie campaign. The origins of this dispute, as Dervla Murphy points out in her admirably balanced account, long preceded the article in an obscure right-wing journal, the *Salisbury Review*, which made Ray Honeyford, headmaster of Drummond Middle School in Bradford, a household name in Britain.

In April 1980 Honeyford, an advocate of traditional 'Christian' values, found himself in charge of a school whose pupils were mostly Asian, the great majority of them Muslims (eventually the number of whites in the school would dwindle to around ten per cent). Soon after his appointment Bradford Council – his employers – launched a programme of anti-racism and multi-culturalism with which Honeyford strongly disagreed, seeing in it an obstacle to the academic advancement of children from all backgrounds. The headmaster aired his objections in a number of articles in *The Times*, *The Times Educational Supplement*, the *Yorkshire Post*, the *Head Teachers' Review* and the *Salisbury Review*. The Council was already highly irritated with Honeyford when the contents of an article by him in this last publication – an intellectual quarterly of the right edited by the ultra-conservative philosopher Professor Roger Scruton – was 'picked up' by the *Yorkshire Post*. Honeyford had expressed his resentment against being required by the Council to offer *halal* meat twice a week in school, by stating that the English regarded the manner of slaughter as cruel. This was a highly contentious issue. Animal rights activists had joined with the racist National Front in condemning *halal* killing as cruel: yet as both Muslims and Jews have often pointed out, ritual slaughter is considerably less cruel than the lifetime incarceration of animals by factory farmers.

The main source of annoyance which appears to have inspired Honeyford's article in the *Salisbury Review* was the habit Asian parents had of taking their children on visits to the subcontinent during term time. Unfortunately, he allowed his well-intentioned concern for the academic welfare of his pupils to spill over into a generalised attack on Pakistan. The country was corrupt at every level; it was 'the heroin capital of the world'; it was ruled by a military dictator who – in the opinion of at least half his countrymen – had had his predecessor judicially murdered. Honeyford ended his article by asking, 'How could the denizens of such a country so wildly and implacably resent the simple British requirement on all parents to send children to school regularly?'[25]

The *Yorkshire Post*'s revelation enraged a significant number of parents, race relations workers and influential Muslims, including Sher Azam of the Council of Mosques. Copies of the offending passages in Honeyford's article were circulated, appropriately translated; a protest group, the Drummond Parents' Action Committee, was formed and more than two hundred parents – over half the total – signed a letter to the Education Committee demanding Honeyford's dismissal. The action committee quickly learned how to dramatise its demands: before the nation's press and television cameras, it set up an alternative school at the Pakistani Community Centre which nearly half the pupils attended. The Council was unnerved: after a six-hour debate the Education Sub-Committee passed a vote of 'no confidence' in Mr Honeyford, empowering the Director of Education to dismiss him.

By now Honeyford had become a national figure: for the left and activists in the Asian community, he was a 'racist'; for the right, a martyr to the cause of freedom of speech. Honeyford's union, the National Association of Head Teachers, threatened to block any move to dismiss him. White Bradfordians collected 10,000 signatures for a pro-Honeyford petition to Sir Keith Joseph, the Education Secretary. The Conservative MP for Shipley, Marcus Fox, was granted an adjournment debate in the House of Commons. The government came out openly on Mr Honeyford's side. In due course, Mrs Thatcher even invited him to Downing Street, to attend a 'private discussion of leading educationalists'. His opponents were depicted in the Tory press as an unholy alliance of Muslim bigots and rabid Trotskyists.[26]

The Council's Education Officer wavered. Honeyford was suspended on full pay pending an inquiry by the school governors. After a four-day hearing, accompanied by massive demonstrations outside the school, a narrow majority of governors voted to reinstate him for a probationary period. His union's insistence that reinstatement should be unconditional was upheld by the High Court. Honeyford's return to his school under police escort in the face of noisy protests by parents, some boycotting pupils and the anti-racists made the headlines and the national television bulletins. The Bradford community was becoming dangerously polarised: apart from the small group of left-wing anti-racists, most whites were pro-Honeyford.

'Who the fuck do they think they are trying to run our schools? There's no bloody schools where they come from!' was a not untypical reaction.[27] The Muslim Lord Mayor of Bradford, Mohammad Ajeeb, received a bundle of obscene hate mail after breaking his vow of silence and criticising the Council for reinstating Honeyford.

The anti-Honeyford protesters were just as extreme: some of the banners were almost as vicious as those which appeared in the anti-Rushdie agitation three years later: as well as posters reading 'Honeyford Out!' and 'Ray-CIST' the headmaster was depicted, as Rushdie would be, as a devil with horns under the legend 'Honeyford writes with the blood of Blacks – DEVIL OUT!'

Even more striking was the appearance of themes that would re-emerge, with the volume turned up several notches, during the Rushdie agitation. 'Honeyford has insulted us!' was the constant refrain that Dervla Murphy heard from Mirpuris in Bradford: 'His reinstatement was seen as yet another "insult" to their community.' She concludes with an observation that was highly acute when it was published, two years before more than a handful of Bradford Muslims had heard of Salman Rushdie. In retrospect it has the ring of foreknowledge:

It is difficult to take this kind of thing seriously in modern England, where an insult is no longer a matter of life and death. We may feel resentful or vengeful or take libel or slander action. But we don't think of washing away the blood stains on our honour. Some Mirpuris do. To them a man who has insulted their religion, parents, community and country

is a *legitimate* target. And this is a deep-rooted tradition, not
the sort that withers within a generation or two of settling in
the more temperate climate of England. On more than one
occasion newly arrived immigrants have been knifed to death
to avenge insults inflicted twenty or thirty years ago in Azad
Kashmir.[28]

At first the activists, backed by the left, intimidated many Asian
pupils into boycotting the school. The Council warned parents
whose children failed to attend that they could face prosecution;
after that all but a hundred-odd children turned up, braving
the picket line. The Drummond Parents' Action Committee
responded by organising a strike of all the city's schools.
Although only a quarter of Bradford's 16,000 Muslim pupils
took part, tension in the city remained extremely high. The
protesters' anger was heightened by the school board's decision
to co-opt three pro-Honeyford governors, confirming the headmaster in office. Asian youngsters – encouraged, according to
some reports, by the far left – looked menacing. Only delicate
police handling and the toughness of the Muslim stewards
prevented serious riots from breaking out.

The crisis was eventually resolved after the Appeal Court
overturned the High Court's decision, ruling that the Council's
statutory duty to provide education for the children in their
area gave them the ultimate power of dismissal. Honeyford –
who had been on sick leave – was persuaded to retire early
after accepting a substantial redundancy package, the largest
settlement ever awarded to a teacher in the state sector.

There seems little doubt, from Dervla Murphy's account, that
Honeyford was the wrong man for the job: he was tactless and
insensitive in a post where tact and sensitivity were essential.
But the charge of racism is harder to make stick. Honeyford
was clearly genuine in his concern for the educational welfare
of his pupils. To be opposed to multiculturalist education is
not the same as being racist. Honeyford's critics on the left
deliberately ignored this difficulty for reasons of political opportunism.

Multiculturalism is a game that needs at least two sides – the
'home team' and the 'visitors'. It is entirely desirable that the

home team, in accordance with traditions of hospitality, should make newcomers feel welcome. It is parochial and insulting, for example, to pretend in a school where ninety per cent of pupils come from the Indian subcontinent, that history began in 1066 (or 44 BC); to teach only Christianity in religious education classes; to ignore, in science history, the important contribution of Arab and Muslim scientists to development of the scientific revolutions of the West. From my own experience as a school governor I know that some educationalists, however dedicated, are Christian bigots who find the whole concept of multiculturalism inherently objectionable. Similar attitudes persist in local government: a survey of British local authority attitudes towards Muslim needs elicited this response from the chief executive of one district council who – as well as revealing a poor command of English grammar – informed the researcher he was replying to his questions

> merely to supply the information and not in any way to support this study. The reason I say this is that Muslims have an anti-Christian attitude and, in many parts of the world, are responsible for and promote persecution of Christians. I therefore consider that it is wrong to promote relations with these other religions in this country unless they were clearly with the intention of conversion to Christianity. There is far too much other religions in this country and belittling of Christianity.'[29]

The issue of religious education is particularly sensitive: in the current climate, it seems almost insoluble. Thus in 1985 the Swann inquiry into multi-ethnic education endorsed a 'non-denominational and undogmatic approach' to RE in order to enable pupils from all religious backgrounds 'to understand the nature of religious belief, the religious dimension of human experience and the plurality of faiths in contemporary Britain'.[30]

In effect the Swann Committee suggested that religion should be taught from a perspective of cultural relativism or even, dare one suggest it, of 'epistemological doubt'. The problem, of course, as any teacher of Muslims would recognise, was that this admirably objective approach runs directly counter to the widely held Muslim belief in the superiority of Islam over all other faiths. For example, a handbook entitled *Guidelines and Syllabus on Islamic Education*, issued by the Union of Muslim Organisations for teachers of British Muslim children, addresses the need to teach other faiths in the following words:

As students at this stage are going to be confronted with the problem of realizing in what way Islam is superior to all other religions and ideologies, in what way it is the most liberal as well as the most comprehensive way of life, how it is the most orthodox and at the same time the most advanced form of ideal, they should be allowed to compare Islam with other forms of religion and all new ideologies, especially the humanistic ideology of Humanism and Marxism.[31]

As Professor Hulmes points out, if the *Guidelines* reflect 'the general approach to education of many influential Muslims' as well as the 'wishes and aspirations of Muslim parents for their children in British schools, it is clear that the declared aims of pluralism and of multi-culture education are contrary to Muslim expectations'.[32]

It takes more than one to play multiculturalism.

CHAPTER FOUR
Conspiracy

I visited Bradford in June 1989, nearly a month after the demonstration I had witnessed in Hyde Park. My first appointment
was with Sher Azam, chairman of the Council for Mosques.
Since Bradford had Burned the Book in a blaze of publicity in
January, Mr Azam had become a national figure. His office was
in a slightly run-down semi-detached Victorian house near the
University. It had once been the home of Frederick Delius, the
composer, whose father had been a prosperous wood merchant.
The plaster was crumbling in places and the window had been
boarded up: vandals who had suddenly discovered the virtues
of post-modernist fiction had broken in, daubing the walls
with pro-Rushdie slogans. The Council of Mosques had been
established in 1980, partly on the City Council's initiative: with
so many mosques under the control of different Islamic factions,
the authority had wanted a single body to deal with. Sher Azam
had been a natural choice for President. Previously he had been
President of the Muslim Association of Bradford, running the
central mosque. He had dealt with the urban authority, passing
on complaints about the bussing of children to schools in
outlying districts and the lack of *halal* meat.

Twenty-two of Bradford's twenty-six mosques were represented on the Council. About half of them were under Deobandi control; ten were Barelwis, with one each for the
Ahl-i-Hadith, the Shi'a and the Ismaili Bohras. In addition
to the mosques, eighteen other Muslim organisations were
represented. Each mosque and organisation had two seats on
the Council. They made voluntary contributions in addition to
an affiliation fee of £25 a year. 'We don't receive any other

funding or finance from any government outside the UK,' said Mr Azam emphatically. This did not exclude the possibility that individual mosques, including the two controlled by the Jamaat-i-Islami, had been given funds from abroad.

Mr Azam's voice was soft and lilting, an appealing mixture of Yorkshire and Pakistan. His long, thin face was fringed by an Abraham Lincoln beard: he seemed the image of a patriarch, a man in his prime. In some ways, he had to admit, Salman Rushdie had done the Muslim community a favour: 'We used to have questions about where we are and what is going to be our future. Now action committees have been formed in every city up and down the country.' In the past there had been difficulties, given the community's fragmentation. People would continue to worship in their own mosques, to follow their own *tariqas*. But now at least there was an organisation that could provide a platform for all of them. Soon they would be able to select delegates who would speak for the whole Muslim community in Britain.

'This will be useful for the future. Muslims are becoming much more united,' said Mr Azam with more than a hint of pride in his voice: Bradford was definitely on the Islamic map, a Mecca of the north. 'The next generation, the third generation which is now coming up are calling themselves Muslims, not Pakistanis or Asians. They are speaking English, their culture is British, and they are Muslims. What it means, of course, is that we have decided to stay here in Britain. We have to be able to discuss the common issues facing the whole British Muslim community. In the past people went home and then found they had to come back again for economic reasons, following which their families joined them here. Now people have no intention of returning to Pakistan. Our children are not going to go anywhere, unless they are thrown out.'

Like Ulster Catholics in 1969, whose demand for 'civil rights' – for equality in housing and local government – represented a tacit acknowledgement that they were part of the United Kingdom (something their parents had turned their backs upon), the Muslim demand for equality in protection against blasphemy represented a back-handed compliment to Britain and its values.

Algerians in France were unsure of their status, uncertain of their rights as citizens; Turks and Moroccans in Germany, like Spaniards or Italians from the *mezzogiorno* in Switzerland, were still 'guest workers', fodder for the hotels or assembly lines who would return to their families sporting expensive clothes, spouses or motor vehicles, but insufficiently secure in their rights as *citizens* to make demands of the state. The outsider who wants to be recognised, not as a surrogate insider, but in his own right, makes demands which, consciously or otherwise, he knows it will cost the state dear to concede. Catholics, pressing for parliamentary representation, demanded formal acknowledgement that the Glorious Revolution of 1688, foundation of the English Constitution, was religiously partisan and therefore incomplete; Jews a *de facto* acknowledgement that the state was no longer 'Christian'; Muslims, building on these earlier victories of toleration, demanded something which deliberately transgressed the implicit secularism of those earlier victories: a privileged position in the market place of ideas, a demand that their peculiar shibboleths should be rendered taboo.

'Islam is the religion of free speech,' said Mr Azam. It was true up to a point: my experience of the Muslim world suggested that speech was a good deal freer than writing, a not unusual situation in mainly oral cultures where literacy carries the prestige of power and is consequently politicised. Mr Azam went on to discourse on the loss of moral values consequent on the decline of Christianity. The failure of the Church, he said, was really a matter of presentation. Church doctrines were so encrusted with dogmas that the people had deserted. But now the pendulum had swung so far away from religion that by solving one problem many others had been created. Loss of moral values, marriage breakdown, home lives shattered, drug abuse, people ending up in homes, all these things could be put down to loss of faith.

'I can be fairly objective and say, if people believed in religion, many of these problems would be resolved,' said Mr Azam. It was a familiar argument, one often heard from American Protestants who seemed unaware that prostitution, gin-shops, syphilis and child exploitation were just as prevalent in the days of Hogarth and Rowlandson, when religion was in full swing, as any contemporary evil: religion unless harnessed to social and institutional change achieved nothing. 'So if you abandon religion you're going to have more problems. You cannot allow Islam to be attacked and still have freedom. We live in a global culture now. The whole world has to learn to live in peace and harmony.'

'But how does *The Satanic Verses* attack people's beliefs?' I asked. 'Nobody is compelled to buy a book; indeed, if it hadn't been for the book burning, many fewer people would have read it.'

'The people would have become aware of it,' said Mr Azam. 'Islam don't have a priesthood. Therefore every Muslim is responsible for his own acts, his own beliefs. Nowadays it's so easy for ideas to travel from one end of the world to the other. Your book can be published in London one day, tomorrow it's available in all major cities of the world. People will have access to it, regardless of publicity.'

'It's a difficult book and comparatively few people would have read it. Anyway, how did you come to hear about it? I don't believe it's the sort of book that you would normally read . . .'

'We received letters from the Hizb ul Ulama in Blackburn at the end of September enclosing extracts from two Indian magazines; we also received cuttings from a Bradford man who had read the articles in India . . .'

'So you didn't hear about the book till it had been banned in India?'

'A Muslim teacher in Leeds told me it was an awful book. At first I thought it was one of those general complaints one hears all the time. But I asked two colleagues who are interested in books to read it. We held our discussions in private: *we did not give it any more publicity than was absolutely necessary*. But then our members began to write more and more indignant letters to us . . .'

Mr Azam explained that portions of the book had been translated into Urdu so that the local *ulema* – qualified authorities on Islamic Law – could decide if it was blasphemous. They were unanimous that the book attacked Islam.

'But it's a work of fiction,' I said. 'You have to see the book as a whole, not just bits out of context.'

'You have to look at the author's intention.'

'You mean in the book or outside the book?'

'Outside the book. It's clear his attitude to Islam is hostile. There have been interviews, articles in the press.'

With hindsight it is easy to see that there was no way the Muslims of Britain could have been insulated from *The Satanic Verses*. The book was highly controversial even before its publication – not in Britain, but in India, Rushdie's country of origin. Several weeks before its appearance in Britain Khushwant Singh, a distinguished Indian journalist who acts as an editorial adviser to Penguin Books India, read the book in typescript. 'I read the manuscript very carefully, and was positive it would cauŝe a lot of trouble,' Singh told Chitrita Banerji of the magazine *Sunday*.[1] 'There are several derogatory references to the Prophet and the Qur'an. Muhammad is made out to be a small-time impostor.' Singh conveyed his doubts directly to Peter Mayer, Chairman of the Penguin Group, in several telephone conversations. According to Singh, Mayer was 'quite appalled' at his reaction. But any idea that Penguin's Indian subsidiary would publish the book under its own imprint was quickly abandoned.

Singh's warning that the book would almost certainly be banned by the Indian government was soon borne out. On 5 October *The Satanic Verses* was placed on the proscribed list by the Ministry of Justice, acting on orders from the Prime Minister. Rajiv Gandhi had been alerted by a letter from an influential MP, Syed Shahabuddin, a member of the opposition Janata party who liked to present himself as a champion of India's 100 million-strong Muslim minority. Although considered 'something of a liberal' by the standards of Indian Islam, Shahabuddin is under constant pressure from Deobandi hardliners such as the powerful Sayyid Abdullah Bukhari, Imam of the main mosque in Delhi. Shahabuddin played a leading part in orchestrating Muslim agitation against a court decision granting Hindus access to the shrine of Ayodhya in Uttar Pradesh. Ayodhya, known to Hindus as Rak Janma Bhoomi and to the Muslims as Babri Masjid, is considered in Hindu tradition to be the birthplace of the god Ram. A mosque erected there by the Mughal Emperor Babur (1483–1530) became a symbol of Islamic conquest. Muslims took the court's redress of this ancient sacrilege as an insult to their community: Mr Shahabuddin called it a 'death sentence'.[2]

Shahabuddin had not read *The Satanic Verses*. 'I do not have to wade through a filthy drain to know what filth is,' he wrote in an article in *The Times of India* two weeks after the ban. Commenting on the chorus of liberal outrage that greeted the ban, Shahabuddin hinted at the pressures that were building up in the Muslim community:

> The élite do not understand the dynamics of mass communi-cation – how reports spread and how rumours, sometimes exaggerated and wild, fly and take possession of the minds of men. Translations, excerpts in various languages, com-ments in the local press, editorial reviews and, over and above them all, interviews (the most inflammatory being brave statements by the writer himself) percolate down to form an emotional torrent and, given the religious context, reason and restraint are swept away in the current of passion.[3]

The network of Muslim outrage appears to have been activated by two interviews Rushdie gave in Indian magazines: in *India Today* he explained to Madhu Jain that 'the image out of which the book grew was of the prophet going to the mountain and not being able to tell the difference between the angel and the devil'[4]; he rejected Shrabani Basu's suggestion in *Sunday* that the book should be banned because of the delicate communal situation in India. In retrospect his remark is extraordinary, revealing either a breath-taking naïveté or a perverse refusal to face up to Indian social realities: '. . . it would be absurd to think that a book can cause riots. That's a strange sort of view of the world.'[5]

Shahabuddin pointed out, among the polemics, that Rushdie's book would in any case be liable to prosecution under Article 295A of the Indian penal code which states, *inter alia*, 'Whoever, with deliberate and malicious intention of outraging the religious feelings of any class of citizens of India, by words either spoken or written or . . . otherwise, insults or attempts to insult the religion or the religious beliefs of that class, shall be punished with imprisonment . . . or with a fine . . . or with both.'[6]

Article 295A had been added to the penal code by the British after an incident that found many echoes in the affair of *The Satanic Verses*. In 1924 Rajpal, a Lahore bookseller, published a book in Urdu entitled *Rangila Rasul* (*The Merry Prophet*), which implied that Muhammad's life and revelation had been intimately linked to his relationships with women. The author was subsequently murdered by two young Muslims, who in turn were sentenced to death, making them martyrs for the whole Indian Muslim community. Not having powers to ban the book, the British authorities prosecuted the publishers for inciting religious hatred. After three years of evidence and counter-evidence Rajpal was eventually found guilty and sentenced to eighteen months' rigorous imprisonment, only to be freed by the Lahore High Court, presided over by Mr Justice Dalap Singh, a Christian. Ten thousand Muslims had attended a protest meeting in Lahore; the governor of the Punjab, William Hailey, responded by banning any further public meetings. When Muslims disobeyed the order Hailey met a delegation, promising that if necessary the government would amend the law to prevent circulation of material that was 'blatantly offensive' to religious feelings. Muslim anger was exacerbated, however, when contempt of court charges were brought against a number of newspapers that had commented adversely on Justice Dalap Singh's judgement. Hailey decided that only a successful prosecution would calm them down. A special branch was set up to hear arguments against the author of a hostile essay on Muhammad published in a Hindu newspaper under the title 'A Trip to Hell' – which gave a Dantesque account of the Prophet's torments. To the government's relief the judges ruled against the journal's editors and publishers. It was after this incident that, following Hailey's advice, the Government of India drafted amendment 295A making it an offence to 'insult or outrage the religious feelings of any class'.[7]

Not that Article 295A always protected the hyper-sensitivities of India's Muslims. Another far more serious episode following a supposed insult to the Prophet occurred as recently as 1986. In December of that year a Bangalore newspaper, the *Deccan Herald*, published an English version of a short story by P. K. N. Namboodiri, originally printed in the Malayalam language without incident some ten years previously. Entitled 'Mohammad the Idiot', the story was about a deaf mute who commits suicide after being abused and made drunk by some ruffians. Although the story makes it clear that Mohammad is the victim of human spite, generated in part by communal rivalry and 'theological one-upmanship', in which Hindus were as culpable as Muslims, Muslim mobs immediately went on the rampage, wrecking buses and shops in central Bangalore. An apology immediately issued by the newspaper's editor and publishers, plastered on posters all over the city, did nothing to quell the disturbances, which spread to neighbouring Mysore, inspiring counter-riots by Hindu mobs, who attacked defenceless Muslim women and children in their huts. By the time order had been restored sixteen people had been killed in the riots, all of them by police firing into the crowd. Dozens of people were injured and millions of rupees' worth of property damaged. From accounts in the Indian press,[8] the initial wrath of the Muslims was aroused not by the content of the story, but its title, exacerbated by the fact that the names of two of the Prophet's relatives (his father Abdullah and his mother Amina) occur in the text. As a reporter on the *Indian Express*, V. N. Subba Rao, observed: 'It was as if some unseen old wounds had been suddenly reopened, even as the city reacted with disbelief and shock.'

No doubt Rajiv Gandhi's motives in banning the book were partly political: with a general election due in November 1989, he could not afford to alienate the Muslim vote. But it is difficult to see how he could have acted differently. India is a religious powder keg. Although Indian Muslims had won concessions by having Islamic family law enacted in parliament, they had yet to adjust fully to the psychic trauma of being a minority in a Hindu-dominated *jahiliya* state. In a democracy, however corrupt its leaders or flawed its institutions, it was inevitable that people would seek political advantage by fanning the

flames of intolerance. Rushdie's interviews, his very choice of
title, had already created the impression that his novel 'insulted'
Islam. In Bangalore people had died because of a newspaper
headline. In the circumstances, it is a moot point whether
Shahabuddin was stirring things up or trying to calm them
down.

What, in retrospect, seems absurd, is not the all too obvious,
if unpalatable, fact that an item of fiction can cause rioting and
death in India, but that a novelist whose reputation has been
built on his grasp of the Indian psyche appeared to think
otherwise. Yet in his combative response to the Indian ban
Rushdie seemed blissfully unaware of the realities. In his first
'open letter' to Rajiv Gandhi, published in various newspapers,
the novelist took the Prime Minister to task for giving into
religious pressures:

From where I sit, Mr Gandhi, it looks very much as if your
Government has become unable or unwilling to resist pressure from more or less any extremist religious grouping, that,
in short, it's the fundamentalists who now control the political
agenda in India. You know, as I know, that Mr Shahabuddin,
Mr Kurshid Alam Khan, Mr Suleiman Seit and their allies
don't really care about my novel one way or the other. The
real issue is, who is to get the Muslim vote? I deeply resent
my book being used as a political football, and what should
matter to you more than my resentment is that you come out
of this looking not only philistine and anti-democratic but
opportunistic and that's bad.

Mr Prime Minister, I can't bring myself to address finance
ministries about literature. In my view, this is now a matter
between you and me. I ask you this straightforward question:
What sort of India do you wish to govern? Is it to be an open,
or a repressive society? Your action in the matter of *The Satanic
Verses* will be for many people around the world, an important
indicator. If you confirm the ban, I'm afraid I, and many
others, will have to assume the worst . . .[9]

In an article written for *The Illustrated Weekly of India* after the
government upheld the ban, Rushdie's indignation exploded

into a fit of rage that revealed the same combustible mixture of insecurity and arrogance that characterised his enemies:

> So there is now a new member of the philistine conspiracy . . . I accuse Mr Gandhi of playing at communalist politics for narrow electoral advantage; and I offer him a terrible possibility. Mr Prime Minister, *The Satanic Verses* may just, in the eyes of the world, be the unmaking of you. Worse still is the judgment of the eye of eternity . . . and, Mr Gandhi, has it struck you that I may be your posterity? Perhaps you feel that by banning my fourth novel you are taking a long-overdue revenge for the treatment of your mother in my second; but can you be sure that Indira Gandhi's reputation will endure better and longer than *Midnight's Children*? Are you certain that the cultural history of India will deal kindly with the enemies of *The Satanic Verses*? You own the present, Mr Gandhi; but the centuries belong to art.[10]

Sher Azam's colleague at the Council of Mosques, Liaqat Hussein, confirmed that the first intimations of the book had come from India. He showed me a copy of the circular from Blackburn, printed in English and Urdu. The document was undated, but since it referred to the Indian government's ban it must have been written after 5 October. It mentioned two articles in Indian newspapers, one by Shahid Sidiqi of *Nai Duniya*, from Delhi; the other by Abdul Kadir Meer of the fortnightly *Umeed* from Surat. Mr Sidiqi's article stated: 'The novel writes about an Indian film star named Gibril Farishta who is supposedly a reincarnation of the Prophet Mohammed. Makkah sharif is called "Jahiliya (evil city)" . . . The author of this book also mentions "The devil's synonym Mohoud" [*sic* which means, satan's other name Mohammed (God forgive us and punish him).'

Abdul Kadir Meer's account treads the same ground:

> The murtad [apostate] Salman Rushdie tried to say that the prophet Mohammed did not recognise [i.e. distinguish between] Wahee [revelation – i.e. the Qur'an as the talk of Allah or Satan (Allah forgive us and punish him). The author

. . . names Madina Sharif as 'Yathrab' [*sic* and mothers of UMMAT (wives of the prophet Mohammed S.A.W) as prostitutes . . . Salman Rushdie should understand that people like him who have criticised Islam have long gone, without even affecting Islam. Islam continues to rise day by day and night by night.

The circular is clearly sincere in its horror of what it supposes the book to contain. It urges people who have 'purchased this satanic novel to either destroy it or return it to us. *Please don't attempt to read or buy this satanic novel* [emphasis added]. Wherever possible gather in crowds and force these places not to sell such rubbish pleadingly.' The circular concludes by urging the imams of all mosques to organise petitions at Friday prayers to be sent to the Queen, the Prime Minister and the Home Office, and that photocopies should be sent to all Muslims, especially students.

A letter from Sher Azam to the Prime Minister, Margaret Thatcher, dated 12 November, contains similar phrasing and refers to the same two Indian publications. Significantly, it contains no hint of the wording of a statement issued by the Islamic Foundation of Leicester. That statement, signed by the director, Dr M. M. Ahsan, was carried in the 14 October issue of *Impact International*, a Muslim weekly published in London. Dr Ahsan's version, as would be expected, is considerably more literate in English than that of the Blackburn *ulema*:

With deep anguish and distress we are writing this note to draw your attention to the recently published blasphemous novel *The Satanic Verses* (Viking, 1988). This work, thinly disguised as a piece of literature, not only grossly distorts the Islamic history in general, but also betrays in the worst possible colours the very characters of the prophet Ibrahim and the Prophet Muhammad (peace be upon them). The Prophet (peace be upon him) is referred to in this novel as 'Mahound' – an insulting name meaning 'devil' or 'pagan god' coined for the Prophet by the medieval West. The work also disfigures the characters of the Prophet's Companions (Bilal, Salman Farsi, Hamza, Abu Sufyan, Hind, Khalid and several others – may Allah be pleased with them) and the Prophet's holy wives: and describes the Islamic creed and rituals in the most foul language.[11]

The initiative in this case seems to have come from Jamaati-i-Islami activists in India. According to *The Illustrated Weekly of India*, Ahmed Ejaz of the Islamic Foundation in Madras informed his friend Faiyazuddin Ahmed, recently arrived at the Foundation's centre in Leicester, about the Indian government's stand. They decided to try to get the book banned in Britain by putting pressure on Muslim governments through the Islamic Conference Organisation and Saudi Arabia.[12] It was reasonable for them to assume that Saudi pressure would be effective. The Saudi government had been partially successful in having the controversial film *Death of a Princess* – which alleged that Saudi princesses were in the habit of transgressing the desert kingdom's rigid sexual code – withdrawn from several European television networks. It could safely be assumed that the self-styled 'Guardian of the Two Holy Shrines' – as King Fahad now preferred to call himself – would have no trouble persuading Western governments and the Pearson Group, the owners of Penguin, to act over Rushdie's book. The Maududists and their allies deliberately raised the temperature of the protest by publicising the offending passages. The issue of *Impact International* dated 28 October devoted seven pages to Rushdie and his book. It included a page full of quotations most likely to outrage believing Muslims, and a list giving the page numbers of other passages too lengthy to be included. There is a hostile profile of 'Simon Rushton aka Salman Rushdie, anti-Islam's new find', based on a rather tendentious summary of three profiles published earlier in the national press. The article begins by describing the difficulties Rushdie had eating kippers at Rugby ('apparently he had had no trouble with pork, ham or bacon'), when none of his snobbish British schoolfellows would help him. This searing experience determined the young Indian to 'show them all'. Ever since that time his career had been 'a continuous striptease, from soft to hard and even harder porn'. Following the success of *Midnight's Children*,

He had hoped to win the Booker Prize once more. He was cross when he did not and set about putting together his *Satanic Verses*. Combining all his skills in writing, acting and imagining and remembering his credo 'I will show them all' he has achieved an enormous success in outrage and sacrilege. If he does not get the Booker Prize a second time this year, he can look forward to winning the Nobel Prize, next year or the year after that. There is no reason to assume that he is incapable of producing something yet more filthy than his *Satanic Verses*.

The laboured sarcasm is authentic Maududism: Rushdie will surely win the Nobel Prize because everything Western is rotten and corrupt. In his main article introducing the offending blasphemies, *Impact*'s editor, M. H. Faruqi, attacks the Muslim intelligentsia for failing to withstand the assaults of academic orientalism:

The earlier corps of missionary orientalists has since been fortified by a later arrival of Zionists [*sic* orientalists and now we are beginning to have Hindu 'experts of Islam'. The Muslim response to this intellectual development has less to do with setting their own house in order, protecting their own political and intellectual sovereignty and building and strengthening their institutions of learning . . . On official plane [*sic* Muslim institutions and authorities bend over back-wards to appease the very same experts [by helping draft Islamic family laws approved by various governments].

Faruqi describes Rushdie in terms very similar to those applied by Zionist extremists to Jewish critics of Israel: he is 'a self-hating Indo-Anglian, totally alienated from his culture, who has also learnt that it is possible to make money by selling self-hate'. Rushdie's response to Muslim criticism is rejected out of hand: 'Faced with the rising anger of the Muslim community Rushdie was now saying "How could I be anti-Muslim when my whole family is Muslim?" Absolute rubbish. To be a traitor one has to belong to the community one intends to betray.'

The fictional context in which the offending passages occur is dismissed with equal vigour:

It was painful in the extreme to reproduce some excerpts from his *Satanic Verses* but whatever the context they were absolutely profane and blasphemous . . . It matters little if this entire sequence happens in a dream, fictional dream, of a fictional character, because here we are dealing with the creator of that so-called fiction. Fiction and fantasy are no licence for insult and profanity. A deranged mind can dream any dream but the moment he begins to insult and provoke then he enters the no-go area . . . As long as such fantasy is confined to one's private thoughts or even writings, there would be little cause for anyone to concern himself with it, except the person's own psychiatrist. But to publish illiterate sacrilege and to try to make money out of it on the excuse that it is a work of great literary merit, is not acceptable . . . The fact is that apart from making money out of sacrilege, Rushdie would also like to subvert Islamic values so that no one can point a finger at his 'secular' way of life . . .

Significantly, in his recommendations to the Muslim community Faruqi refrains from urging an extension of the blasphemy laws – which, had they been applicable to *The Satanic Verses*, would certainly have applied to his article: as the *Gay News* case revealed, intention is not a defence in law. Instead he contents himself with reporting the demands to Penguin to withdraw and pulp the book, to offer an unqualified apology to the world Muslim community and to pay damages equivalent to the returns from copies already sold; pending such action Penguin/Viking assets in Muslim countries should be frozen, while educational titles should be exempted from copyright. Faruqi concludes by adding, somewhat wistfully, 'Perhaps it would be more salutary if the author is allowed to enter into Islamic jurisdiction and prosecuted under relevant law' – one which, presumably, would carry the death sentence. Faruqi, however, warns the Muslims whose fury he has been so careful to stoke against taking the law into their own hands: 'Leave Mr Salman Rushdie all to himself and to his charmed circle of "literary friends". We have to say this because we also sense a milling anger about the outrage committed by him' – anger, one might add, which Mr Faruqi was doing his utmost to stir up.

The Maududist campaign was predictably successful. Dr Salem Azzam, Secretary General of the Islamic Council of Europe, telexed the Ministers of Information of all the Muslim countries, urging them to ban the book, a request with which most of them complied in due course. One of the first countries to ban the book formally was South Africa, which has a substantial Muslim population. In November Rushdie was obliged to cancel a speaking engagement after his hosts had withdrawn their invitation. Dr Azzam described the novel as 'a deliberate attempt in collusion with the enemies of Islam to ridicule the teachings and practices of Islam, the Prophet, his wives and companions'. A UK Action Committee, representing the Council of Mosques, the UK Islamic Mission (a Jamaati-controlled organisation), the Union of Muslim Organisations (recipient of funds from the Saudi-backed World Islamic League), the Maududist Islamic Foundation, and several other organisations was formed at the Central Mosque in Regent's Park. Its convenor was Dr Mughram al Ghamdi, director of the Islamic Cultural Centre. In his circular dated 28 October – which carried considerable weight, coming as it might have seemed from the British equivalent of al Azhar – Dr al Ghamdi incorporated a whole paragraph from that issued by Dr Ahsan of the Islamic Foundation a fortnight earlier: 'This work, thinly disguised as a piece of literature . . . the most foul language'. The same paragraph was included *in toto* in the statement released by the South African government early in November explaining its reasons for banning the book.[13]

Dr al Ghamdi added a further hyperbolic twist by stating, with all the authority at his command, 'This is the most offensive, filthy and abusive book ever written by any hostile enemy of Islam . . .' More filthy than Dante? More abusive of Muhammad than the medieval miracle plays? The hyperbole emanating from the Central London Mosque contrasted with the comparative moderation and literary *savoir faire* I encountered in Bradford: there were people there who thought the book should be withdrawn, not because 'this was the most filthy and offensive book ever written by any hostile enemy of Islam', but because certain passages had 'gone too far'. For example, both Anwar – whom we shall encounter in due course – and Ishtiaq Hussein, a local authority worker, had admired Rushdie's earlier works, and were prepared to concede that *The Satanic Verses* had excellent literary qualities: their reservations were confined to specific passages, notably the brothel scene, which, they felt, went 'over the top'. Even Dr Shabbir Akhtar, the leading 'fundamentalist' intellectual, acknowledges Rushdie's 'fine insight' into aspects of Indian family life, and the 'profound insight into the dangers of a false religion' he reveals in his treatment of the Hawkes Bay incident.[14]

The statements issuing out of the Central London Mosque were disastrous for the image of Islam in Britain. Whereas the pleas of semi-literate Pakistanis could be viewed, by liberals and other well-intentioned people, with compassion, the anathemas issuing from Regent's Park were both menacing and wholly lacking in intellectual credibility. While it was possible for people of good will to sympathise with the wounded feeling of British immigrants who were often economically disadvantaged and suffered from racial attacks, the impression given by Dr al Ghamdi and his colleagues was that the Islamic leadership in Britain was ignorant, intolerant, philistine and out of touch with political, social and legal realities. This ineptitude, reinforced by the knowledge that the salaries of Dr al Ghamdi and his colleagues were paid for by a government where churches are forbidden and even classical works of Islamic theology are banned for religious reasons, did much to damage any sympathy the British government and media might have developed towards the Islamic case.

An example of Muslim perversity was provided by one of the men who became prominent in the campaign, Hesham el Essawy, a Harley Street dentist who chaired an organisation calling itself 'The Islamic Society for the Promotion of Religious Tolerance in the UK'. In his letter to Penguin dated 12 October, Mr el Essawy showed himself incapable of distinguishing between history and historical fiction as literary forms: 'I question the right of anyone to falsify established historical record, albeit in a novel or otherwise . . .' Mr Essawy had evidently never read the novels of Walter Scott, Stendhal, Tolstoy, not to mention Margaret Irwin and other popular writers, in which real people like Saladin or Napoleon encounter fictional characters, contrary to 'the established historical record'. A record is only 'falsified' if the work in question purports to be factual. Mr el Essawy's conclusion was equally naïve: 'To sanction such a work,' he wrote, 'is to invite agonies and disasters from which none of us will be safe, we might as well knight muggers and give mass murderers the Nobel prize.' Penguin executives must have wondered what world Mr el Essawy had been living in: had he never heard of Kissinger of Cambodia, or Begin of Deir Yassin?

On arriving in Bradford I expected to find confirmation that Jamaati circulars had inspired the militancy in that city – that the Jamaat had lit the spark that led to the Burning of the Book. However, if the Bradford campaign had a Jaamati provenance, it had been very cleverly concealed. Had the Jamaat been involved in the initial stages, one would have expected phrases from Dr Ahsan's circulars to have found their way into Sher Azam's letter to the Prime Minister. As it was, the element of undergraduate arrogance ('this work, thinly disguised as a piece of literature') was missing; instead a tone of astonished outrage seeped through the very imperfect English, creating the impression of genuine hurt.

Honourable Madam:
   The Muslims of Bradford and all over the world are shocked to hear about the Novel called 'SATANIC VERSES' in which the writer Salman Rushdi [*sic* has attacked our beloved Prophet Mohammed PBUH and his wives using such dirty language which no any Muslim can tolerate . . . We as a [*sic* Muslims will never allow or ignore such rubbish words used by a person who is either mad or thinks that he is ruling the whole world in which there are Millions of Muslims. We are very much distressed when we came to know about the author living in Great Britain and the publishers too. As citizens of this great country, we have expressed our very ill

feelings about such harmful novel and its publishers and state that the novel should be banned immediatly [*sic* . . .

Mr Azam said he hadn't received the circular from the Regent's Park Mosque till after he had written to Viking. 'Afterwards,' he said, 'we found that many other Islamic institutions had done the same, without each others' knowledge.'

'So the whole thing built up spontaneously?'

'We was very hurt. Had it been the concern of an individual or one particular organisation – from one city or area – we might have put up with it. But then we found out that many other Islamic foundations without the knowledge of each other had already written to Penguin. We was angry and upset, because we found out that there was a whole lot of different organisations protesting, and they were doing nothing about it.'

Mr Azam was convinced that Penguin had published the book for money. Their profits had been dwindling. Insulting Islam was proving a good way of improving the balance sheet. There may have been political reasons as well.

'Penguin was aware of what they was doing. Whether they did it out of greed, or out of pressure from the Jewish lobby, or what, they did not do it out of freedom of speech,' he said, when I ventured to suggest that Penguin had bought the book because they were convinced of its literary excellence.

'Are you thinking perhaps that it was part of some kind of conspiracy against Islam?' – thinking of some of the posters I had seen at the demonstration in London.

'Oh surely.'

'You feel that it was part of a deliberate attempt to undermine Islam?'

'It would be wrong of me to say I'm one hundred per cent convinced. The people who have the information have started to convince me that it was a conspiracy, but at the moment we are not sure who is behind it. Call them "anti-Islamic forces". That is a very broad statement, but that is what we are agreed upon.'

I got up to leave, but he suddenly checked me.

'I'll tell you one more thing. The other day somebody asked me outright: "Will the Muslims kill Rushdie or not?" And I said: "Look at it, he's kept well away, in secret, from the Muslims. The only people with access to him are the so-called Friends of Salman Rushdie, the anti-Muslim lobbyists. Any time these people might be exposed. To avoid exposure they will kill Rushdie, before he comes out of hiding. That will be their last effort, so that he cannot speak."' '

'When you say the Friends of Salman Rushdie, are these the people who you say are behind the conspiracy?' I knew the Friends. Most of them weren't friends of Rushdie in the personal sense: they were lobbyists for freedom of speech, upholders of Article 19 of the UN Charter. The Chairman, Kevin Boyle, was an Irish law professor whom I had known for many years. So far as I knew there was nothing anti-Muslim about him. One of the activists, John Hoyland, I had also known distantly for more than a decade: he was a writer of left-wing libertarian views, but not, so far as I could tell, anti-Muslim in any specific sense – though, like myself, he was not well disposed towards religious fundamentalism.

'Some, perhaps,' said Mr Azam. 'They are anti-Islam, anti-Islamic forces. Because if this come out, if it gets into the hands of the Muslims, if they find out who is behind Rushdie and what he has gone through, the anti-Muslim lobby will be exposed. And we will have conclusive evidences from what you call horse's mouth. We expect it will be the anti-Islamic lobby that will kill him before he comes out.'

'But what is this anti-Muslim lobby? Who is behind it?'

'We'll have to wait and see.'

The conspiracy theory was widely held in Bradford. Liaqat Hussein, of the Jamiaat Tabligh ul Islam, thought there was an anti-Islamic lobby throughout the Western world, spearheaded by the Jews.

'You have only to look at the statement of writers supporting Rushdie,' said Mr Hussein. 'Almost a third of them are Jews.'

I pointed out that quite a few Jewish writers, like Susan Sontag, Norman Mailer and Philip Roth, were against book-burning and blasphemy laws for the same reasons as Salman Rushdie – they had rejected the religion into which they had been born. Religious Jews in Britain had not attacked the Mus-

lims – the Chief Rabbi had been more supportive of their case
than many Christians. Mr Hussein and his colleagues seemed
unconvinced. That they would suspect a plot, a conspiracy of
malignant forces ranged against Islam, was, I suppose, inevitable. In a sense it flattered Muslim self-esteem that Islam
should be the target of such a conspiracy, whether organised
by Jews in revenge for Muslim resistance in Palestine or by
Christians carrying on the Crusades. For several years British
Muslims had been told by intellectuals they trusted that 'Islam'
and 'the West' were two mutually exclusive, mutually hostile
systems, that the whole thrust of Western civilisation was
hell-bent on destroying Islam. 'The western civilisation is funda-
mentally an immoral civilisation,' writes Dr Kalim Siddiqui of
the pro-Iranian Muslim Institute, echoing Maududi and Qutb:

> Its 'values' are free of moral constraints. Indeed, such moral
> values as survived the Christian experience were systemati-
> cally eradicated. Such a civilisation, when it acquired physical
> control over traditionally Islamic societies, set about eradicat-
> ing the moral values of Islam as well. Those parts of our
> societies that the west has succeeded in disintegrating from
> the highly integrated Islamic social order all display the same
> symptoms of corporate selfishness and a shift away from
> moral behaviour. The nation-state is the ultimate instrument
> of corporate immorality, followed closely by the political
> party.[15]

Islamic fundamentalism, like fascism, holds out the vision of a
'fully integrated' society free from damaging divisions of class
and wealth – a society which is presumed to have existed in
the golden age before Western colonialism entered the picture.
Like fascism, it seeks a psychological foundation in absolute
certainty: the only difference being that instead of the Will of
the Leader, it relies on the Will of God, as imparted through
His representatives on earth or as revealed in His Book. The
fundamentalist mentality – absolutist, anti-democratic and
highly authoritarian – is prone to see conspiracies where none
exist: as Steve Bruce points out in connection with the 'New
Christian Right' in America, it is entirely consistent with an

orthodox religious viewpoint in which life's 'apparently inexplicable vicissitudes' are explained in terms of God's providences on the one hand and the manipulations of the devil (or a 'Satanic West') on the other.[16]

Moreover, embedded in the generalised anti-Western thrust of fundamentalist discourse there exists a specific anti-semitic thread. In theory Muslim writers, like non-Muslim critics of Israel, distinguish between a specific critique of Zionism and a generalised hostility towards Jewish people. Not to do so, after all, would amount to an acknowledgement of the Zionist claim – eagerly promoted by the Israeli government – that no distinction exists, or ought to exist, between Jews, Zionists and the state of Israel, and that the latter represents the whole 'Jewish people'. Such distinctions, however, are not always maintained in practice. Thus the writings of an influential British convert to Islam, Dr James Dickie (who usually writes under his adopted Muslim name, Yacoub Zaki), reveal a consistent tendency to cross the line between anti-Zionism and anti-semitism – for example by appearing to endorse the neo-Nazi view of the Holocaust as a 'myth'.[17] Some years ago I myself was outraged when a leading Muslim intellectual offered *The Protocols of the Elders of Zion*, the notorious Tsarist forgery circulated by the Nazis, as 'proof' of the Jewish conspiracy to rule the world. If educated writers like Dr Dickie revealed anti-semitic tendencies, it was hardly surprising that such attitudes were to be found among Mr Hussein and his friends in Bradford.

The conspiracy theory – of which the anti-Jewish version is one of the archetypes – had some plausibility in the absence of rational explanations. Jews were prominent in publishing; Jews supported the Israeli occupation of Muslim lands. Ergo *The Satanic Verses* was part of some wider movement directed against Islam. Why else would the British government refuse to do what was so obviously in its interest – to force Penguin to withdraw the book?

I tried to explain that Rushdie had broken no law, and that in Britain the government had no powers to force Penguin to withdraw his book.

'What about *Spycatcher*?' said my interlocutors. I explained, as patiently as I could, that the government had sought to prove

to the satisfaction of the courts that Peter Wright's book violated
an existing law – an argument it eventually lost in the House
of Lords. They listened politely, but sounded unconvinced.

'Mrs Thatcher has admitted the book is offensive. The Home
Secretary should order its withdrawal.'

Under the Raj these things had been handled much more
firmly – under Section 295A. I suspected that there was a
subtext to the campaign in Britain: the row was really about
inter-communal relations between Muslims and Hindus in
India, with British Muslims unconsciously projecting the fears
they inherited from their subcontinental experiences on to their
British host community. British Muslims had inherited from
their colonised past the assumption that the government ought
to protect them, as a minority, from the insults of the Hindu
majority; that, after all, had been a part of the Raj's *raison d'être*:
from the Olympian heights of their cultural and administrative
superiority, the British had kept the peace – a peace which
collapsed into devastating communal tensions as soon as they
announced their intention to leave. Colonialism fosters dependence. For the Mirpuris and Campbellpuris, the Pathans,
Punjabis, Azad Kashmiris, Bengalis, Pushtus and Gujeratis
who made up the highly diverse communities of British Islam,
running to Nanny Raj crying 'he hit me', with the expectation
of redress, was the most natural thing in the world.

Nor did the protesters get anywhere with Penguin. 'Penguin
refused to acknowledge the offence,' said Mr Hussein. The
publishers had indeed stuck to their guns: what else could they
do? Their letters to the various Muslim protesters were polite,
but firm:

We wish to make it clear that, despite a number of requests
from Islamic organisations and members of the public to
withdraw Salman Rushdie's novel from sale, we cannot do
this. To do so would be wholly inconsistent with our position
as a serious publisher who believes in freedom of expression
. . . We are truly sorry for the distress the book has caused
you and some of your fellow-Muslims, but we feel your
reaction is based on a misreading of the book . . . we stand

by our view that this is a fine literary novel, a view that has been fully endorsed by the critics . . .

Once it had become clear that both Nanny and Penguin were refusing to act, frustration boiled into rage.

'In November we had our first meeting,' said Mr Hussein. 'That's when we decided to hold a public meeting in the Pakistani community hall. But nobody reported it. We weren't being heard. Someone suggested we should hold a larger meeting in one of the Bradford University halls. Then we decided to hold the meeting outside the hall because we knew that if it was held indoors, no one would take any notice. That's when we decided to burn the book.'

'Whose idea was it, to burn the book?'

Mr Hussein could not remember. He thought it was the imam of one of the mosques. He actually went and bought a copy for the purpose. Then Sayyid Abdul Quddus, a member of the Council of Mosques, did some advance publicity. He told the *Telegraph and Argus* about the demonstration. The strategy worked. It was the public relations coup of the decade.

Abdul Quddus did the honours: the brown Yorkshireman, tweed overcoated and hatted, the picture of outraged respectability or fascist bigotry, depending on one's point of view, put a match to the book after it had duly been doused in lighter fluid the better to conflagrate. It made a beautiful image, an icon of iconoclastic rage, the perfect emblem for the Rage of Islam, on film, on video, in colour stills, in black and white.

'All the newspapers commented,' said Mr Hussein proudly. '*Times, Daily Telegraph, Guardian, Yorkshire Post*. They compared us to Hitler!'

'That was unfair,' I said. 'Hitler never wore a hat like Mr Abdul Quddus.' •

CHAPTER FIVE

Ayatollahs of the North

Actually, *The Times* didn't compare Mr Adbul Quddus to Hitler. Hitler does not loom large in Islamic demonology: there is not much reason why he should. Nor is he the universal hero among Muslims that some Zionists assume him to be. The Muslims were divided during the Second World War over whether to support the British devil they knew against the Nazi devil they didn't. Generally enthusiasm for the Nazis diminished with proximity to Axis power: there was considerably more in Iraq than in Libya. Palestine, of course, was a complicating factor: it is undeniable that some Muslim leaders, like Hajj Amin al Husseini, were prepared to collaborate with Hitler against the British: but so, for that matter, were some of the Zionists, who took the view that founding the Jewish state took precedence over rescuing Jewish lives.

The book burning, however, did put Bradford in the headlines, the media having overlooked a similar demonstration in Bolton six weeks previously. The Honeyford affair had taught Bradfordian Muslims how to capture attention, and it was with that affair that a *Times* editorial drew comparison: the Bradford headmaster had been removed, said *The Times*, because he had stressed the learning problems experienced by the English minority in his school resulting from the stress on Asian culture and language. British Muslims must not try to override the will of the democratically elected government. A remarkable piece by Anthony Burgess told *Daily Mail* readers how Heinrich Heine had responded to the Nazis with his famous statement that those who start by burning books end by burning men and women. More interesting, however, than the disappearance of seventy-five years between the German poet's death and the Nazis coming to power (more likely to have been caused by a malfunction in one of the *Mail*'s subeditors than any lapse of erudition on the part of Mr Burgess) was the backing down by the Central London Mosque. Dr al Ghamdi complained that the campaign he had helped to fuel had been 'hijacked by mischief-makers'; Mr el Essawy talked darkly about the 'sleeping demons of racialism' being awakened. Mr Faruqi of *Impact* wrote a windy riposte to an article by the Education Secretary, Kenneth Baker, who condemned the book burning, insisting that Muslims must put 'argument before arson'. In the course of his article, which gave a résumé of the book's offending passages – just in case any of his readers had missed the earlier number of *Impact*, and had yet to experience the hurt – Mr Faruqi moved closer towards a position of self-indictment by arguing that the absence of laws protecting Islam from blasphemy left the Muslims legally helpless in what was basically a moral issue.

A large demonstration of Muslims in London on 30 January organised by a previously unheard-of group, the Islamic Defence Council, delivered a memorandum to Penguin's offices in Kensington. After complaining that it did not find Penguin's argument in favour of the book 'relevant', it went on to itemise a number of the 'insults' in bold print, as follows:

The books calls Abraham, the revered Prophet of Jews, Christians, Muslims alike, 'the bastard.'

The Blessed Prophet Muhammad is given the Middle Ages' name of 'Mahound' (The word means 'devil' or a 'false Prophet').

He is a man who 'had no time for scruples':

He was 'no angel, you understand . . . !'

The revelations he received were 'well-timed' to suit him when 'the faithful were disputing'.

His companions are described as 'bum' and 'scum'.

The namesakes of his wives are sited in a brothel with all the literary pornography that would go with such a locale.

The Islamic Holy City of Makkah is a city of 'Jahilia' – of ignorance and darkness.

The Muslim 'God . . . sounded so much like a businessman' and 'the Islamic Shari'ah was about every damn thing'.

Sodomy and the missionary position were approved by the archangel.

There is no reference, of course, to the fictional context, beyond the general statement that a defence on these lines is not relevant and the rather quaint statement that it is 'not obligatory to pocket such outrageous insult because one had not wasted his time (and money) on reading this book "in its entirety".' No serious publisher, says the memorandum, 'can take shelter behind the undisputed right of freedom of expression in order to publish such dirty work'.[1] What is interesting about this memorandum, when contrasted with those originally circulated by the Muslims of Burnley and Bradford, is its readiness to flirt with the book's alleged blasphemies – if not to go the whole hog by repeating them verbatim. As the campaign became more organised, so the protesters' outrage became less convincing. The sincerity of the earliest circulars could be gauged from the fact that the writers dared not reproduce the blasphemies for fear of hurting their fellow-Muslims. Once the campaign became organised, and more politically conscious, this self-denying ordinance, entirely logical if one believes that words can genuinely hurt, was abandoned. The taboo had been broken by *Impact*. One could argue that its treatment of the alleged blasphemies was much more hurtful to genuine believers than Rushdie's. They appeared in a magazine that cost only fifty pence, not buried in a 550-page book costing £12.95; instead of having to be extrapolated from the shells of literary make-believe, like crab-meat from a claw, they were carefully pre-packaged, laid out on a single page. The Maududists and their allies – the literate, articulate 'Islamist' ideologues – seemed less concerned to protect Muslim sensibilities than to increase the scale of the agitation in order to bring it under fundamentalist control.

For by now it was becoming clear that the issue was spilling far outside the Indo-British axis – the individual threads of personal connection that linked Mirpur to Bradford, Leicester to Madras. Ever since the Iranian revolution of 1979, Saudi Arabia and Iran, two wings of Islam, two rival orthodoxies, two regional superpowers possessed of oil wealth and modern weapons, had been caught up in a struggle for hegemony in the Middle East, a struggle whose sideplay involved a contest for power over Muslim hearts and minds all over the world. Iran had lost the first round, the eight-year-long Gulf War, which had cost it millions of lives in a fruitless struggle to export its revolution by overthrowing the 'Satanic' regime of the Iraqi dictator Saddam Hussein. In 1988 Ayatollah Khomeini had urged his countrymen to 'swallow poison' and accept defeat – suitably dressed up in the form of United Nations resolutions – at the hand of Iraq, backed by Saudi Arabia and the Gulf States. The contest had shifted to Afghanistan, where the victory of the Muslim *mujahideen* against the Soviets had produced, not the hoped-for Islamic Republican government in Kabul, but a deadlock among the different guerrilla factions, exacerbated by Saudi–Iranian rivalry.

In Pakistan, the situation was particularly delicate. Here the recently elected government of Benazir Bhutto was under growing pressure from the opposition Islamic Democratic Alliance (IDA), of which the Jamaat-i-Islami was a small but influential component. Although Ms Bhutto's Pakistan People's Party (PPP) had emerged as the largest party in the parliamentary elections in November, her room for manoeuvre was extremely limited, squeezed as her government was between a military determined to hang on to the privileges it had acquired during the years of military rule, and the IDA, keen as ever to

use the 'Islamic card' to discredit her. The Jamaatis were smarting from a double failure: in the elections they had only won
three seats; while a parliamentary walk-out they had staged to
protest against Ms Bhutto's confirmation as Prime Minister by
the National Assembly, on the ground that an Islamic state
could not be governed by a woman, had failed to win enough
support to prevent Ms Bhutto from becoming Pakistan's first
female head of government.

The demonstrations against *The Satanic Verses* in Islamabad
are widely believed to have been organised by the Jamaatis,
as were subsequent demonstrations in Bombay, Kashmir and
Dacca. There was no logical motive for them, since Pakistan
had quickly followed India's lead in banning the book in October. Ms Bhutto was right to question their sincerity: was the
protest 'genuine', she had asked, or was it 'really a protest
by those people who lost the election, or those people who
(benefited from) martial law, to try to destabilise the process of
democracy? The dying order always likes to give a few kicks
before it goes to rest.'[2] The ostensible reason for the protest in
Islamabad was the forthcoming publication of *The Satanic Verses*
in the United States, due on 15 February. An angry Jamaati-led
mob of more than 2,000 protesters tried to storm the US Em-
bassy in Islamabad, throwing stones and bricks at police who
were guarding the building, to shouts of 'Allahu Akbar' and
'American dogs!' Police repeatedly fired into the crowd with
rifles, semi-automatic weapons and pump-action shotguns.
By the end of the day, at least five people had been killed
and more than a hundred injured. Television pictures of
these, the first fatalities in the Rushdie Affair, were shown
all over the world, including Iran, capital of the Islamic
Republic.

The Satanic Verses had not gone unnoticed in the Islamic
Republic. In December *Kayhan Farangi*, a literary journal from
the house of Tehran's leading newspaper, published a review
which, compared to the statements circulated by the Jamaati-i-
Islami and the UK Action Committee in London, was surprisingly mild in tone. It pointed out that both *Midnight's Children*
and *Shame* had been translated into Farsi. Indeed, the translation
of *Shame* had won its translator the award for the best translation

of the year. The review was certainly highly unfavourable. *The Satanic Verses*, it says,

> contains a number of false interpretations about Islam and gives wrong portrayals of the Qur'an and the Prophet Muhammad. It also draws a caricature-like and distorted image of Islamic principles which lacks even the slightest artistic credentials . . . Rushdie has fallen from the grace of a writer with a good knowledge of Islam to something like total moral degradation.[3]

There is no suggestion, however, that the author has apostasised from Islam or that his 'distorted images' amount to blasphemy. The article reports the banning of the book in India and the fact that in Britain the 'concerned authorities' have assured the country's Muslim population, which it puts at one and a half million, that they are doing all they can to 'reject' it – a reference, presumably, to the campaign which by then was well under way. It cites a statement by Rushdie on Indian radio in which he accuses 'a bunch of Islamic fundamentalists' of being responsible for the banning of his book in India, curtailing his freedom of expression. It concludes by presenting Rushdie's defence in a surprisingly dispassionate manner:

> Rushdie insists that his book is nothing more than a work of imagination which tries to investigate the birth of a major religion from the point of view of a secular individual. In his view, in the next Indian general election it will be of the utmost importance who can win the hearts and minds of the 100 million Muslims and he believes his book has become a ball in this political game.[4]

Unlike India, Pakistan, Saudi Arabia, South Africa and many other countries, Iran did not formally ban the book, although it was not, of course, available: there was no law, apparently, to prevent an individual importing a copy through customs. Translations are vetted by the Supreme Guardianship Council, an institution established by Khomeini to veto legislation not compatible with the Shari'a; but compared to most Arab countries, there are few restrictions on works in foreign languages.

Meanwhile, the Ayatollah was dying and the revolution he had headed was evidently on the retreat. Ever since Khomeini had swallowed the 'poisoned chalice' of defeat in the shape of UN Security Council Resolution 598 calling for a ceasefire in the Gulf war, the eighty-six-year-old Imam's health had continued to decline: his condition was now widely regarded as terminal. In the ultimate course of things God might still be on the Iranian side; but He had temporarily allowed the 'Satanic' forces of Iraq to destroy Iran's superiority in manpower and morale by the liberal use of chemical weapons. The economy was in ruins; but with hostilities suspended, the exigencies of war no longer provided the excuse for food shortages and astronomical prices. The demise of the Guardian of the Revolution, now expected at any time, led to an increasingly open struggle between the men he had elevated to power and who wanted to stay there. The game was played, Iranian-style, by the rivals trying to outdo each other in pious self-criticism. The radicals, led by Prime Minister Hussein Moussavi and Khomeini's son Ahmed – who hoped his father would place kinship above principles – lamented that the earnings of the country's richest ten per cent had risen steadily as compared with those of the poorest since 1980 – a stark admission of failure in a state that set much store by redressing the balance between the 'oppressed' and their 'oppressors'. The more pragmatic elements, led by Ali Hashemi Rafsanjani, speaker of the parliament and commander-in-chief, denounced the 'shortsightedness, the excesses, the crude aspects' of a foreign policy which had only 'made enemies of ourselves' and took the opportunity provided by peace to push for improved relations with the West.[5]

Early in February M. Roland Dumas, the French Foreign Minister, visited Tehran – the first by such a senior French official since the Revolution; Mr Ali Akbar Velyati, the Iranian Foreign Minister, met the British Foreign Secretary, Sir Geoffrey Howe, in London for talks that were described as 'encouraging'; diplomatic moves were in the air which, it was hoped, could lead to the release of Western hostages in Lebanon as well as the unfortunate Roger Cooper, a British businessman and Farsi-speaker who had been held for three years in Tehran on espionage charges. The Iranians, for their part, expected economic and technological benefits, in the shape of new cars, roads and railways. There were growing signs of liberalisation within the country as well. Classical and folk music – long forbidden as Western or corrupting distractions that diverted the believers' thoughts away from God – had reappeared on radio and television. Women, who had previously been hounded by street morality squads if they wore anything other than the full-length black *chador*, were beginning to appear with brightly coloured headscarves, revealing glimpses of well-permed hair, not to mention make-up.

All such signs of a breeze of change infuriated the radicals, who did what they could to undermine them. Their most effective tactic was to try to draw the Old Man's attention to any departures from the strict puritanism that had been the hallmark of his long and exemplary life. Thus on 7 February the *Guardian of Islam*, the house magazine of the theological seminary at Qom where the Ayatollah had taught for most of his career, denounced the 'debauchery and libertinism' on radio and television. It appeared to refer to an incident earlier in the week when a female interviewee had dared to indicate her preference for the female star of a Japanese soap opera over Fatima, the Prophet's daughter, as a role model. The woman had pointed out that Fatima – a revered figure among the Shi'ites, being the wife of the first Imam Ali and mother of the second, Hussein – had lived 1400 years ago; while doubtless an admirable person, she could hardly be considered more relevant to the life of a modern woman than the star of *Oshin*, a series about the trials and tribulations of a young woman in wartime Japan.

In a letter to the head of Iranian broadcasting, the Ayatollah decreed that if such a slur on the Prophet's daughter had been deliberate, then those responsible for the programme should be executed for blasphemy. Fortunately for them an Islamic court ruled that there had been no malicious intent. Tehran Radio's director of broadcasting and three of his colleagues were found guilty on lesser charges of seriously misrepresenting the views of Iranian women. They were sentenced to between four or five years' imprisonment in addition to fifty lashes apiece; but after an appeal by the Chief Justice, Khomeini relented and agreed that the four could return to work with a warning. The outcome was a partial victory for the radicals, who had checked what they saw as dangerously permissive tendencies on radio and television; but the liberals (the term, of course, is relative) had been spared to 'fight another day'. It was no accident that the man who headed the whole broadcasting network, and most probably the radicals' real target, was Rafsanjani's brother.

For the radicals, checked in their aims by the continuing confidence the Ayatollah appeared to have in Rafsanjani, the Islamabad killings came as a godsend. Some reports state that it was Ahmed Khomeini who brought the book to the Ayatollah's attention; others that he was alerted by a request for a *fatwa* by a group of British Muslims. Whatever the truth, it is certain that once blood had been shed, the Ayatollah would have learned about it. The *fatwa* pronounced on Rushdie, though widely described as a 'sentence of death', was really a legal ruling issued, as such rulings usually are, in response to a question:

> I would like to inform all the intrepid Muslims in the world that the author of the book entitled *The Satanic Verses*, which has been compiled, printed and published in opposition to Islam, the prophet and the Qur'an, as well as those publishers who were aware of its contents, have been declared *madhur el dam* (i.e. those whose blood must be shed). I call on all zealous Muslims to execute them quickly, wherever they find them, so that no one will dare to insult Islam again. Whoever is killed in this path will be regarded as a martyr . . .

In terms of Islamic law, as Malcolm Yapp pointed out,[6] Khomeini was going beyond his powers in ordering Rushdie's death. In his capacity as a *mujtahid*, an interpreter of the law, his was only one opinion among other, alternative, possibilities. It was open to those who sought the *fatwa* to consult a different *mujtahid*: they probably went to Khomeini because they knew he would give them the answer they wanted.

Khomeini's followers, however, regarded him as much more than a *mujtahid*, or even the *vilayet e faqih* or Supreme Guardian of the Revolution: for them he was the Imam – in effect, the Messiah of Shi'ite eschatology. Though he made no formal claim to being the Expected One (*al Mahdi*) who would return to bring peace and justice to the world, he allowed his followers to address him by the title 'Imam', which in Shi'ism was tantamount to identifying himself with the Mahdi. The charismatic, theo-political power he had accumulated gave his *fatwa* far more authority than that of any other living *mujtahid*.

Moreover he exceeded the traditional *mujtahid*'s power in another respect, by arrogating to himself the role of judge. Immediately after the *fatwa* was issued, Hojjat-ul-Islam Sheikh Sanei of the Fifth of June Foundation, one of the many Islamic charitable trusts set up after the Revolution, offered a reward of 20 million tumans (about three million dollars) to any Iranian who would 'punish the mercenary [Rushdie] for his arrogance'. (Non-Iranians would get the equivalent of one million dollars.) In London Rushdie and his wife Marianne Wiggins were immediately taken into protective custody, where the author remains to this day.

Rushdie's initial response to the threat on his life had been defiance: it was a further indication, he said, of the 'extraordinary unscrupulousness' of the campaign against his book: 'The novel is not an attack on Islam or any other religion, but an attempt to challenge preconceptions and to examine the conflict between the secular and religious views of the world. Ironically, it is precisely this conflict which has now engulfed the book.'

After a few days' reflection, however, he took a more conciliatory line: there were indications from Tehran that he might be pardoned if he apologised. President Ali Khamenei, generally regarded as one of the pragmatists, had indicated as much at Friday prayers; while in London the Iranian *chargé d'affaires*, Mr Akhundazeh Basti, argued that the *fatwa* was a purely religious ruling, not a political command. In response to these hints Rushdie issued a statement through his agents:

As author of *The Satanic Verses* I recognise that Moslems in many parts of the world are genuinely distressed by the publication of my novel. I profoundly regret the distress that publication has occasioned to sincere followers of Islam.

Living as we do in a world of many faiths this experience has
served to remind us that we must all be conscious of the
sensibilities of others.[7]

Khomeini, however, proved implacable – compounding
Rushdie's distress with humiliation, for the apology had been
dragged out of him too late to carry any conviction. A statement
issued from the Ayatollah's office and broadcast over Tehran
Radio denied reports by the 'colonialist foreign mass media' to
the effect that the death sentence would be lifted if the author
apologised. 'His Holiness Imam Khomeini, may his shadow
continue, has stated: . . . even if Salman Rushdie repents and
becomes the most pious person of this age, it is still the duty
of all Muslims to use all their efforts, wealth and lives to send
him to hell.'[8] Just in case anyone thought the edicts had merely
been issued by underlings using his name, Khomeini made a
personal statement which was duly broadcast over Tehran
Radio. He described the crisis over *The Satanic Verses* as a
godsend which had delivered Iran from a 'naïve foreign policy'
of rapprochement with the West. 'The world of arrogance and
barbarism unveiled its true face of chronic enmity against Islam
in the Rushdie Affair,' he said. Inveighing against 'uncalled for
clemency towards the enemies of God and opponents of the
system', he swore that as long as he lived he would prevent his
government from falling into the hands of liberals. Western
arrogance would not force Iran to 'forgo the implementation of
God's decree'.[9]

The effect of Khomeini's edict was an immediate escalation
of the crisis. What had started as a campaign in the subcontinent
and Britain spread, for a period at least, throughout the Islamic
world. Ten thousand demonstrated against the book in Iran,
thousands more in Dacca. In Rushdie's native Bombay ten more
people were killed when police opened fire on demonstrators
who had marched against the British Council. Indian intelli-
gence suspected Iranian hands behind the movement, working
through such previously unheard-of organisations as the Muslim Integration Council. Some Muslim leaders jumped on the
Khomeinist bandwagon: the Imam Bukhari of the Delhi Mosque
gave the edict 'one hundred per cent support' – adding, for

balance, that the death penalty should also be applied to Bagh-wan Shree Rajneesh, the flamboyant guru of Poona, for deroga-tory remarks he had made about Krishna. Syed Shahabuddin was more equivocal: 'I have no personal views concerning the *fatwa*,' he said. 'I neither approve nor disapprove of it.'[10] Another leading cleric, Manlan Hasan Ali Nadiri, normally an opponent of Khomeini, endorsed the *fatwa* as 'just and appropriate'. *Ulema* who endorsed the *fatwa* outside the subcon-tinent included the Mufti of the Al Aqsa mosque in Jerusalem and Sheikh Shaban, leader of the Sunni Tawhid movement in Lebanon. Muslim governments, anxious not to be seen drag-ging their feet, issued anti-Rushdie statements and announced that they had banned the book. Even the Communist govern-ment of Kabul, which had just lost its Soviet shield, announced that the book had been banned. There were demonstrations in France and Germany as networks of Khomeini sympathisers among the immigrant population were activated; in Italy, when it was pointed out that Dante had also 'insulted' the Prophet, there were repeated threats to blow up his tomb. Even the normally cautious Muslims in the United States joined in the chorus demanding that the book should be banned.

In Iran the *fatwa* put the pragmatists on the defensive. Since no one could criticise an edict of the Imam, the pragmatists and radicals tried to outflank each other by lauding its virtues and the inestimable service it was doing the Islamic cause. President Khamenei underscored his master's militant wrathfulness by announcing during a state visit to Yugoslavia that an 'arrow' had been launched against Rushdie for his blasphemy. Rafsan-jani, in several lengthy sermons, denounced the 'Zionist con-spiracy' behind the book's publication.

Khomeini's *fatwa*, however, was far from universally recog-nised. What had been intended to unite the Muslims behind Khomeini had the opposite effect, as more worldly leaders examined the implications and counted the cost. Increasingly Muslim leaders, asked if they supported the death sentence, took an equivocal line: while it was true that apostasy carried the death penalty, certain procedures had to be observed. The lead was given by the *mufti* of Egypt, Sheikh Tantawi, who stated that no Muslim could be killed without a full and fair trial: 'The court must ask the writer to explain his intentions and not be limited by misreadings and misunderstandings,' he said. Even if found guilty, he could seek clemency and forgiveness. The moderate tone was reinforced by Abdel Fatah Mourou, secretary-general of the fundamentalist Renaissance Movement in Tunisia. Though a former admirer of Khomeini's revolution, he regarded the *fatwa* as an impious outrage contrary to the spirit of Islam. 'For me,' he told the French magazine *Le Point*, 'Islam does not kill people for their ideas . . . I can't understand why they are making so much fuss about Rushdie when hundreds of writers have written similar things without having *fatwa*s pronounced against them.' While pointing out that there had been no demonstrations against the book either in Tunisia or Egypt, he nevertheless declined to make his position public in Tunisia for fear of stirring things up.

Despite the attempts by the Khomeinists and their allies in the Indian subcontinent and elsewhere to present Rushdie's blasphemies as having attacked 'a thousand million Muslims', it soon became evident that the Muslim world at large was more or less indifferent. Arabs, more secure in their Islamic identities than Iranians or subcontinental Muslims, were less prone to see Rushdie's transgression as an attack on their honour, although, in line with a generally repressive policy towards literature, most governments formally banned the book, ensuring that only those holding diplomatic passports would be able to bring it into their countries.

The leading exception to this picture proved the rule: one of Egypt's leading fundamentalist preachers, the blind Sheikh Umar Abdul Rahman, took the wind out of Rushdie's critics by pronouncing a *fatwa* against the Arab world's leading writer, Neguib Mahfouz, winner of the 1988 Nobel Prize for Literature. If such an edict had been published years ago, said the Sheikh, when Mahfouz's *Children of Gebalawi* came out, Rushdie would never have dared to publish his blasphemies. The bracketing of Rushdie with Mahfouz was highly embarrassing to Rushdie's more sophisticated critics in Britain, who had tried to avoid the charge of philistinism and anti-intellectualism by arguing that Rushdie's insults and calumnies were of a completely different order from Mahfouz's sceptical allegory.

The death blow to the internationalisation of the campaign against *The Satanic Verses* would eventually be struck by the very people who had been indirectly responsible for fanning the fires at the beginning: the Saudis. A conference in Mecca sponsored by the Saudi-funded World Muslim League on 28 February, two weeks after the *fatwa*, signally failed to endorse the Ayatollah's death sentence, although it described Rushdie as a 'heretic and renegade' and demanded that he and his publishers should be tried by the 'relevant courts'. The Saudi position was subsequently spelled out in more detail by the Foreign Minister, Prince Saud. He explained that since religion was not institutionalised in the Islamic world, an insult to a Muslim's religion was perceived as an insult to the community. The present situation could not be defused unless adequate account were taken of the feelings of British Muslims, who would now be looking to Rushdie for genuine signs of repentance. Only the British community among whom Rushdie lived were competent to forgive him. In effect – though of course the Foreign Minister did not spell this out – the Saudis were prepared to 'wash their hands' of the whole affair.

The *coup de grâce* was delivered at the meeting of the Islamic Conference Organisation – consisting of the Foreign Ministers of all the Muslim countries – in Riyadh on 17 March. While declaring Rushdie an apostate and calling for the withdrawal of the book, the conference refused to endorse Khomeini's death sentence. More significantly, this declaration – the least that could be made according to Islamic law – was prepared separately from the conference's main, mandatory resolution, which meant in effect that it was not binding on member states. A delegation of British Muslims, led by Sher Azam, pronounced itself satisfied at the terms of the declaration. But it was no secret that they were bitterly disappointed by the results of their lobbying. They had fully expected to be treated as conquering heroes. Though none would admit it, the Ayatollah had wrecked their campaign.[11]

In the meantime public opinion in the West had worked itself into a frenzy of godless indignation: when bookshops wavered, concerned for the safety of their staffs, writers demonstrated in

the streets, deserting their attics, basements and penthouses to
show solidarity with the beleaguered Rushdie. They delivered
petitions, signed 'World Statements' supporting freedom of
speech, sported 'I am Salman Rushdie' buttons, pledged themselves to die for the cause. European governments, pushed
by the tide of protest, severed what tenuous links had been
established with Iran since the war, when the pragmatists
had seemed to be in the ascendant. Contracts were cancelled,
millions of dollars of business lost. In a vain attempt to appease
Muslim sentiments both Mrs Thatcher and Sir Geoffrey Howe
made their own criticisms of Rushdie's book. Sir Geoffrey told
the BBC World Service: 'The British government, the British
people, don't have any affection for the book, which is extremely critical, rude about us. It compares Britain with Hitler's
Germany. We don't like that any more than people of the
Muslim faith like the attacks on their faith contained in the
book.'

One wonders what ingenious civil servant's memorandum
managed to transform Rushdie's burlesque treatment of Saladin
Chamcha by the immigration squad, or the death in police
custody of Dr Uhuru Simba, the suspected Granny Ripper, who
according to the police, 'fell out of his bunk', into a comparison
between Britain and Nazi Germany, for it is obvious that Sir
Geoffrey hadn't read the book. The statement evidently alarmed
Rushdie, who told Paddy Ashdown, the Democrat leader, that
he feared the British government was about to 'do the dirty' on
him. His fears, however, proved groundless. Within a week
the British government joined with its European partners in
issuing a strong statement unequivocally condemning the *fatwa*
as an 'incitement to murder' which violated 'the most elemen-
tary principles that govern relations among sovereign states'.
British diplomats were withdrawn from Tehran, and the Iranian
chargé d'affaires in London was given his marching orders. The
link was finally severed by the Majlis in Tehran, which formally
broke relations – prompting the criticism that Britain should
have done the breaking first.

From the point of view of community relations, the *fatwa* was
a disaster for the Muslims in Britain. Having painfully, by dint
of hard work and the stoical acceptance of a position low

down the scale of Britain's social hierarchy, created a life for themselves that offered the distant prospect of gradual improvement, they were suddenly thrown into the spotlight. Reporters and television crews invaded schools, homes and mosques, asking tricky questions which few were equipped, by education or training, to answer intelligently – that is to say, with full knowledge of the implications of what they were saying. Very few of those targeted by the media had any training in Islamic law – were even aware of the distinction, crucial to any discussion of Rushdie's fate, that had to be made between *Dar al Islam* and *Dar al Harb*. And the British press is as innocent of ordered, intellectual control, as Islam is of religious hierarchy. Reporters, researchers and producers operate pragmatically, by experience and happenstance, usually under great pressure to produce 'copy' or interviews within the shortest possible time. Experts are rarely employed as advisers in the planning stage: instead they are given time to answer questions or space to air their views in print. The system allows considerable editorial freedom; it also has the remorseless tendency to trivialise, or, where feelings are running high, to polarise. In a crisis which called for delicate handling, in which the broadest possible spectrum of Islamic views should have been represented, the 'hardliners' were given a disproportionate amount of time and space because their utterances made 'better copy'. The impression was given that Muslims in Britain were ignorant, bloodthirsty bigots.

First prize for an Islamic 'own goal' in the media game went to Sayyid Abdul Quddus, hero of the Bradford *auto da fé*, who told reporters he would not hesitate to carry out the death sentence himself: 'Members of our religion throughout the country have sworn to carry out the Ayatollah's wishes should the opportunity arise,' he said.[12] The popular press had a field day. The *Daily Express* reporter had no difficulty in finding 'half a dozen young would-be assassins ready to collect the £2 million bounty placed on Rushdie's balding head'.[13] The Conservative MP Terry Dicks, ignoring the fact that Mr Abdul Quddus was British, demanded that he should be deported. The *Sun* backed Mr Dicks up, with the suggestion that Abdul Quddus be immediately put on the next plane to Tehran.[14]

'They can't be allowed to get away with murder,' screamed the
Star in an offering that sums up the general tenor of the time:

> Isn't the world getting sick of the ranting that pours non-stop
> from the disgusting foam-flecked lips of the Ayatollah
> Khomeini? Clearly this Muslim cleric is stark raving mad.
> And more dangerous than a rabid dog. Surely the tragedy is
> that millions of his misguided and equally potty followers
> believe every word of hatred he hisses through those yellow
> stained teeth. The terrifying thing is not that a lot of these
> crackpots actually live here among us in Britain, but that we
> are actually becoming frightened of them. The whole thing
> is crazy. And it has to stop.[15]

Today urged, less hysterically, that Mr Abdul Quddus be
charged with incitement to murder.[16] West Yorkshire police
said they would seek advice from the Crown Prosecution
Service, which sensibly told them to do nothing: British race
relations were bad enough without creating a martyr for Islam
in Bradford. Mr Abdul Quddus's statement led to a row in the
Council of Mosques of which he was secretary. Mr Abdul
Quddus backed down, claiming that the press had misquoted
him. He was eventually obliged to resign. The Council produced
a conciliatory statement which exhibited a marked increase
in sophistication compared to its previous record. This was
probably due to the active presence of Dr Shabbir Akhtar, a
Cambridge philosophy graduate who had been co-opted on to
the Council as an independent member: 'The Council of
Mosques does not support violence and does not incite Muslims
to break the law of the country in which they live. As an
independent Muslim organisation it does not take any directive
from any institution or government abroad. As Muslims it is
our religious obligation that we respect the law of this country.'

The people I met in Bradford were still smarting from the effects
of the media campaign, which had led to a marked increase in
the number of racial attacks. Yet they also saw the campaign in
support of Rushdie's right to publish in a wider context, as part
of the Western movement against Iran. The leaders of the Arab

countries which had failed to back Iran's line at the Islamic Conference Organisation meeting after the *fatwa* were 'hypocrites'. The Saudis were really heretics, said one of the Muslim leaders, who preferred not to be named. He dwelled on the excesses of the Wahhabite past, when Ibn Saud's warriors conquered Islam's holy places with considerable brutality, smashing the tombs of the Prophet's family and in some cases massacring women and children.

'But surely they are Sunnis?' I said.

'They call themselves Sunnis to save their necks. The things they actually do don't conform to the Sunni way of thinking. But they won't remain in power for long. They are systematically violating the Holy Places. If you ask a genuine Muslim about them, the first thing he'll say is that they've sold out to the Americans. They have no respect for Islam or Islamic values. They have been educated in Western countries and do not reflect the feelings of their own people. It was only Iran which spoke up for the feelings of Muslims,' he added.

'So you would say most people are in favour of the *fatwa*?'

'Almost everybody thinks it is right.'

He wasn't exaggerating: almost all the Muslims I met in Bradford agreed with the *fatwa* in principle. The only real debate was about whether it should be carried out.

'A lot of people don't want to kill Rushdie,' said Muhammad Siddiq, a round and jolly man who ran the Jamaat-i-Tabligh from an early Victorian terraced house in one of the Manningham district's more attractive squares. It was interesting that he put it that way round: it made me feel like an insider . . .

'You mean they wouldn't want to do it themselves, but if someone else did it for them they would think he was getting his just deserts?'

'Yes, I think that's a fair assumption,' said Mr Siddiq. 'If they could get away with killing him without getting caught, anybody would go out and do it. But there are some people who would do it whether they were caught or not.'

Since the Abdul Quddus fiasco, however, the Bradfordians had learned to be more careful of their public image. Their most impressive asset in this respect was Dr Shabbir Akhtar, the 'fundamentalist' intellectual. I knew Dr Shabbir Akhtar by reputation. He had frequently appeared on television defending the Islamic corner in the discussion programmes that followed in the wake of the *fatwa*. Being by far the best educated and most articulate of the 'Bradford Ayatollahs', it was not surprising that he had been co-opted on to the Bradford Council of Mosques as an independent. Having read his defence of Islam's 'militant wrathfulness' in the *Guardian*, I expected to find him somewhat prickly, like so many of the earnest young militants of the Islamic movement with whom I used to have dealings in the days when I worked for an Islamic magazine. He turned out to be earnest, friendly and engaging.

Despite his credentials, I had not been greatly impressed by his defence of 'militant wrathfulness'. His principal argument was that 'the continual blasphemies against the Christian faith have totally undermined it. Any faith which compromises its internal temper of militant wrath is destined for the dustbin of history, for it can no longer preserve its faithful heritage in the face of the corrosive influences' of secularity.[17] This argument would certainly have to be greatly refined if applied to Christianity in the United States, where the offence of blasphemy had fallen into complete desuetude, without any appreciable loss of religious fervour. His insistence that 'anyone who fails to be offended by Rushdie's book *ipso facto* ceases to be a Muslim' seemed in my understanding to actually verge on blasphemy: for despite the penalties in Islamic law applied to blasphemers, there existed the view that God alone was judge of a person's belief. It was not just in the Shi'a tradition that the principle of *taqiya* applied, determining that orthopraxis or correct behaviour took precedence over orthodoxy or correct teaching. It was at least debatable whether Rushdie's transgression belonged to the realm of behaviour or doctrine, since a work of literature could be placed in either category. Similarly, for a trained intellectual, Dr Akhtar seemed to have seriously misread the tenor of Rushdie's attack on Islam – if indeed it was an attack at all.

'Rushdie's attack on the authoritative integrity of a fallible Koran,' he wrote, 'is part of a larger indictment of Islam as a faith which routinely and regularly confuses good with evil, divine with diabolic imperative.' On my reading of *The Satanic Verses* it was the practice rather than the faith of Islam that was

Rushdie's target – a wholly legitimate target in a world where twelve-year-old boys were being sent to their deaths by ageing clerics in order to defend, not so much Islam, as clerical power and privilege. 'Militant wrath' had a chilling sound to it: its meaning sent shudders up the spine, conjuring visions of the horrors of the Thirty Years War, the Inquisition, the sectarian poison of Ulster and the horrors of that recent, and wholly unnecessary, slaughter in the Gulf.

Still, there were intriguing aspects of Dr Akhtar's position that made him far more interesting than any of the Islamic fundamentalists whose work I had read. Unlike Maududi with his dismal certainties, painstakingly worked out to transform the globe into a joyless Pakistani *casbah*, where women stayed permanently indoors, Akhtar seemed to allow for the possibility of that most unfundamentalist quality, doubt. 'A Job-like scepticism, reverent and sincere, is found in many Islamic thinkers and novelists, all the way from al-Ghazzali to Muhammad Iqbal and Neguib Mahfouz.' For a man who described himself as a fundamentalist, to defend Mahfouz while condemning Rushdie seemed distinctly odd. For it was not only Sheikh Umar Abdul Rahman and the zealots of the Jihad Movement in Egypt who regarded Mahfouz as an apostate. The view was shared by fundamentalists in Britain, who regarded the Egyptian novelist as a secularist stooge. An article in the fundamentalist weekly *Crescent International*, for example, insinuated that Mahfouz had written his sceptical allegory *Children of Our Alley* purely to curry favour with the Nasser regime in Egypt.[18]

On closer inspection it turned out that Dr Akhtar was not a fundamentalist at all – at least not in any recognised understanding of the word. He was in fact a philosophical theist who sought to defend his belief in the deity by philosophical arguments. Not being a trained philosopher, I was not in any position to judge the skill with which he performed this office. An article of his reprinted from the *Southern Journal of Philosophy* seemed, to my layman's mind, to be argued with lucidity and wit. I had no doubt that had he been born with the right connections, or done his postgraduate work somewhere other than Canada, he would be lecturing students at one of our universities, instead of doing a rather humdrum job in the community relations department of Bradford City Council.

Having investigated, and dismissed, the arguments of various experts in the field, Akhtar concludes that 'all knowledge, including secular knowledge, may indeed be seen as resting on faith'. His defence is explicitly intellectual – something one rarely hears from fundamentalists, who do not generally feel the need to defend revelation from the onslaughts of reason, relying as they do on the authority of the text. Akhtar's article evidenced a personal struggle with doubt, as well as an admiration for 'reverend sceptics' from Job to Nietzsche:

> The religious believer facing a philosophical critique of his religious convictions (especially for the first time) finds that it takes a very short time – if he is reflective – before his religious beliefs are no longer held instinctively. One becomes conscious that they are held *on faith*. A reflective believer finds that if he candidly considers the sceptical objections to his faith, he can no longer retain his intuitive religious convictions unimpaired. After such ordeals, the life of faith requires self-conscious effort; the innocence of one's former pre-philosophical days is irretrievably lost.

It was not therefore the doubt, but the tone in which it was expressed, that offended him about *The Satanic Verses*. In naming his prophet Mahound, Rushdie had deliberately drawn on a reservoir of anti-Islamic Western polemic. The book's popularity in the West invited one to 'look in the region of motives' – both author's and reader's. Like Dr Azam, he was looking outside the text.

'You seem to be clearer than I am about the author's intentions,' I said. 'Isn't that what you would call an *ad hominem* argument, because you are presupposing the author rather than just his text?'

'I'm surprised you think otherwise,' he said. 'The book's such an obvious revival of ancient Christian polemic.'

'I can see how people might read it as an insult,' I said. 'But in order to do so you have to suspend the suspension of disbelief, ignoring the rhetoric of fiction. The passages that have caused most offence occur in the context of a dream in which Gibreel is having a psychotic collapse which subsequently leads to suicide. He is one of the damned.' I then related an anecdote which, admittedly, I had heard at third hand; but it sounded plausible. A senior psychiatrist at a Pakistani hospital had observed that during the Zia dictatorship, which had sought to cover up its nefarious activities by a policy of 'Islamisation', there had been a notable increase in the number of mental patients who had cursed God and His Prophets or other religious figures. A Muslim psychotherapist I consulted, who specialised in patients from different cultures, confirmed the significance of this, explaining that blaspheming during therapy could be a way of getting rid of parental fixations or hang-ups. One of his Catholic patients used to curse the Blessed Virgin in outrageously sexual terms; gradually he transferred the curses to his mother, then to other women, eventually experiencing the release that enabled him for the first time to form healthy relationships. Blasphemy could be therapeutic: indeed some Buddhist therapeutic groups positively encouraged it. The Muslim therapist did not encourage it directly; but he agreed that talk about 'fucking the Virgin' could be beneficial, entailing the release of incestuous feelings. He also admitted treating Muslims who had blasphemed during therapy. One of his patients, an underpaid but highly educated man from a very strict family, had found release in cursing, not the Prophet, but an influential Sufi *pir* in his homeland.

All this seemed to indicate, I argued, that Rushdie, with his extraordinary intuition, had put his finger on a genuine psychological fact. Was it not rather hard on Rushdie to take Gibreel's dreams as representing his authorial voice, rather than the fantasies of a character he had created – a character experiencing the psychic stresses with which the professionals were familiar, and a character, furthermore, who ends by killing himself, becoming, as it were, one of the damned?

Shabbir Akhtar's answer was disappointing. He was a very young man, and I doubted if he had ever considered therapy (though I forbore to ask him): 'I'm not going to deny,' he said, 'that people who defend Rushdie are ingenious enough to put forward arguments of that nature.'

I did not press him in this area, sensing that it either lay outside his range of interest, or that the problems it raised would be too disturbing. I had come to Bradford to listen.

Our discussion moved to less swampy ground. The blasphemy laws should be extended to protect Muslims, said Akhtar. Michael Ignatieff had been wrong to argue that they should be abolished because they were no longer consistent with 'a legal ethos which protects individuals rather than doctrines'.[19] According to the liberal view, it was right for the law to protect women or blacks against racism or sexism, because people were inescapably women or black, femaleness and blackness being biologically determined. It was wrong for the law to protect religious beliefs because they were doctrines involving freedom of choice. But the distinction was not nearly so clear as liberals like Ignatieff maintained. People from time to time took the 'road to Casablanca' to change their genders – not to mention the transvestites, who did the same thing socially and sartorially, if not anatomically. Even 'blackness' was partly a function of ideology, as the 'black is beautiful' brigade testified.

'There's a very contrived sense in which people can't change things about themselves,' said Shabbir. 'What if someone regards his religious belief as wholly necessary to his lifestyle, an integral part of his identity? I think it's highly patronising for someone else to tell him that it isn't. I find it very irritating when liberals tell me that my race and gender are an inescapable part of me, but that my religion isn't. Islam says that man is *homo islamicus* by birth. St Augustine and the early Fathers insisted that knowledge of God is part of human nature, that the only explanation for disbelief is perversity, that people chose to disbelieve what they know. I think Ignatieff's argument, that we should protect people not doctrines, is specious. Of course doctrines don't need protection. Doctrines don't take offence. We protect doctrines because there are people who hold them!'

I was impressed by the force of this argument. Although I have reservations about being *homo islamicus* or indeed *homo christianus* (my religious tendencies being too pantheistic to find accommodation in any form of transcendental monotheism), it remained inescapable that religion for many people was part of their identity, as much as race or gender. The idea of race being

biologically determined, and hence 'inescapable', had been
subverted by the ideology of 'anti-racism', which insists that
virtually anyone not 100 per cent white, whether having African, Arab, subcontinental, South-East Asian, even Chinese
genes in their make-up, should signal their commitment to the
Cause by identifying themselves as 'black'.[20] This was fine as
long as the people concerned thought that racism was best
fought by dividing the world into 'us' and 'them', a view with
which I strongly disagree. But it made nonsense of the biological
determinism on which anti-racist legislation was predicated. It
would be putting it much too strongly to argue that people
were black from choice; but there was no question but that
'blackness' was partly an ideological construction in which
choice was an element. Anyone who has lived in a country
like Egypt knows that in the Islamic world the categories of
blackness and whiteness are subsumed within other categories
– tribal, urban/rural or religious: some Egyptians are dark-
skinned, others as pale as northern Europeans. In Egypt the
blackness and whiteness about which Anglo-Americans agonise
loses its significance as a source of self-identification – which is
not to say that snobbery towards the flat-nosed, crinkly-haired
or darker-skinned is non-existent.

Yet having conceded that religion and race cannot easily be
disentangled, I doubted whether legal protection should be
extended to cover both. Extending the blasphemy laws would
create far more problems than it would solve: Rastafarians
would make the late Emperor Haile Selassie a 'no-go area';
Scientologists would demand the same for L. Ron Hubbard
(surely one of the most bare-faced charlatans in a country that
produces them by the dozen); the Moonies the same for their
leader, the Reverend Sun Yung Moon. For by what criteria
would the law decide on which religions or doctrines should
be protected? All religions begin their careers as cults; only the
God of history determines the true from the false, the genuine
from the fraudulent – which, of course, is one of the themes
one can find in *The Satanic Verses*.

We had supper in an Indian café in the Manningham district,
next to a brand new mosque, eating the curry in our fingers
with chappatis, eastern-style. Shabbir Akhtar discoursed elo-

quently on the double standards operating in British society. The play *Perdition*, which had offended some influential Jews because of its suggestion of Nazi–Zionist collaboration during the Second World War, had been taken off with hardly a breath of protest from outraged liberals; the government had no hesitation in banning or trying to ban publications it did not like, such as *Spycatcher* or the *Observer's* report on the takeover of Harrods by the Al Fayads. But when the Muslims demanded withdrawal of a book which outraged their deepest feelings, all hell broke loose. The whole of the liberal intelligentsia was mobilised against them. In the modern age, Shabbir repeated, 'good must assume militant forms'. Faith must be active; faith must be prepared to sacrifice itself. If the Muslims had been a powerful, well-organised lobby like the Jews, Rushdie's outrages would never have got into print. All of this rang true. I agreed that the double standards over *Perdition* and *Spycatcher* were outrageous, though like most liberals I drew the opposite conclusion: in the interests of fairness, freedoms should be extended, not restricted.

But it was faith, not politics, that aroused his deepest passion. I raised the questions that always trouble me about Islam – questions which evidently troubled Rushdie. If the Qur'an was really, as most Muslims insisted, the 'uncreated' word of God, could he, a Western-educated philosopher, possibly accept that a woman's testimony was worth only half that of a man in court?

'This is a scandal,' he said, 'a scandal of the faith. Like the scandal of Abraham's sacrifice: he left his wife and child in the desert. You have to show you love God above your wife and children. God decrees what He pleases. We have to accept it, that's the scandal of the faith. God's commands sometimes seem impossible: but we are duty-bound to obey. As St Augustine put it, "O Lord God Thou hast counselled a course Thou hast not permitted."'

I was struck by the repertoire of references in which Shabbir dressed up his defence of the faith. His intellectual wardrobe seemed to be filled with exclusively Western clothes. His discourse was replete with references to St Augustine, St Thomas Aquinas, Kierkegaard and Nietzsche; I listened in vain for

Islamic names like Ibn Sina (Avicenna), Al Ashari, al Ghazzali, Ibn Rushd (Averrhoes), Ibn Khaldun or those early Islamic masters, so much more enlightened than Augustine, the Ikhwan al Safa (the Brethren of Purity). It seemed strange that a Muslim who took up the philosophical cudgels in defence of theism should rely so exclusively on arguments put forward by non-Muslim philosophers. I suspected that once he addressed himself to those great Islamic minds he would find his militant wrathfulness tempered by the generosity, scepticism and humanism that were part of their vision. Perhaps, when he had assimilated them, he would find that he was not a 'fundamentalist' after all. I suspected that for all the gifts of reason he demonstrated, his motives were really emotional: he sought to defend what he called fundamentalism out of chivalrousness, out of a desire to empathise with members of his own community, to avoid taking the road that enticed the intellectually gifted sons of Islam into the enemy camp, so to speak. His 'fundamentalism' seemed poles apart from the extremism of Khomeini, Maududi and Sayyid Qutb and their modern exemplars in Britain, Kalim Siddiqui and M. I. Faruqi. But I kept that thought to myself. I had come to Bradford to listen.

Instead, we found ourselves talking about love. Muslim women, he found, lacked humility.

'What do you mean by humility?'

'Young Muslim women are not religiously inclined. I met a girl whom I liked, but when I told her she must repent, she said: "I've done nothing wrong!" so she refused to marry me.'

There was a hint of bitterness in his voice: his faith seemed to be costing him more than was fair. The references to Job were not without significance. For a man of his accomplishments – under thirty, with two highly regarded books of philosophy behind him – he was probably frustrated. He had been turned down by various universities; before he joined the Council's community relations department he had worked as a librarian.

'Are you a man of action at heart?' I asked. 'Do you prefer what you are doing, or would you rather teach philosophy?'

'I don't mind what I do, so long as it's honourable. I wouldn't mind being a priest.' It seemed an odd admission for a champion of Islam. But it sounded true.

'Why is it so important for you to obey the Law of God?' I asked.

'Because I'm a perfectionist.'

'Would your life disintegrate if you didn't keep to the Law?'

'No, I think I would rather enjoy it. I experience temptation like every other normal, healthy male. But I resist it. I have resisted it successfully all my life.'

How impossible it must be, I thought, to take one's religion that seriously. But then, it would only be possible if one believed in the afterlife. As a lapsed Christian, I supposed, I could have it both ways: another Western double standard. No necessity of faith to keep body and soul together – but somewhere deep in one's soul there was the comforting thought that if there turned out to be an afterlife after all, God loves the sinner: the Free Gift was not conditional on ticking the YES box today, before the Special Offer expired.

As we left the café and walked to my car, we passed a white prostitute standing on the pavement. She looked pale under the street light, with fine curving legs stretched out in fishnets from under the miniskirt that barely covered her posterior. Her face, no longer youthful, looked puffy and scarred. If Shabbir had not been with me I would have paid her a fee and listened to her stories about the faithful, about how some of them had trouble performing with wives they had no feeling for, wives chosen by their relatives in Pakistan. It was obvious she was waiting for customers from the café where we had been eating.

There was no scandal to the faith in the services she would render the community that evening; no threat to *izzat* in the back-to-backs. Not all Bradford's Muslims took their religion as seriously as Shabbir Akhtar. 'There is no monkery in Islam,' said the Prophet (Peace Be Upon Him), a prophet who loved nothing more (excepting God) than 'women and sweet odours'. Not all the Bradford Muslims were moral perfectionists who struggled with the flesh and the devil, not to renounce the world, but to conquer it.

CHAPTER SIX

The Word and the Text

I met Anwar at a conference at Bradford and Ickley Community College, one of several held to discuss *The Satanic Verses* in the summer of 1989. The level of discussion was, on the whole, considerably more intelligent than the debates held in television studios in London. The London literati who agreed or volunteered to appear before the cameras shared a crusading outrage at Muslim desecration of the temple of free speech. The Muslims, an odd selection of individuals containing a disproportionate number of European converts, were either too aggressive, or seemed confused, defensive or inarticulate. Although at the Bradford conference there was patently no meeting of minds between Rushdie's critics and defenders, there was real concern on both sides. Bradfordians, regardless of the provenance of their genes, were confronted with the issue in their daily lives, in the streets of their city. For young Asians, 'Salman Rushdie' had become a new racist taunt, a weapon used by skinheads and lager-louts to beat them about the ears and other parts of the body. Their seniors, who worked with white people in local government or business, noticed a distinct chill in the atmosphere after the book burnings and demonstrations – though nothing so un-British as direct verbal reference. The whites at the conference were also genuinely concerned – more so than some of London's literati, who privately expressed a certain glee at Rushdie's incarceration which they felt 'he had coming to him', on account of his hyperbolic unBritishness, his outrageous conceit, his refusal to withdraw his book after the deaths in Islamabad, or the preposterous amounts of publishers' money he had received for writing unreadable prose. In Bradford the whites sensed the very real danger of violence on their streets.

The seminar did not produce anything resembling common ground; but it did define, better than any television programme, the area of conflict, the reason for Muslim hurt. Ian Wright, a lecturer in English, delivered an impressive account of the novel, locating it in the context of contemporary world literature. He explained how the form of 'magic realism' developed by Jorge Luis Borges and Gabriel Garcia Marquez in South America had deliberately subverted the dominant mode of narrative realism – the forms of Jane Austen and George Eliot, Balzac and Flaubert, Turgenev and Tolstoy – by introducing surrealistic events, like people being covered with magic butterflies or characters suddenly enabled to fly. This subversion of narrative form, he argued, had a political dimension: it involved a deliberate, self-conscious attempt to break with the 'cultural imperialism' of European form. He elaborated this thesis into a general description of post-modernist fiction, especially in North America, before moving on to explain Rushdie's satirical ambiguities, the different levels of meaning that could be extrapolated from his text. This lucid exposition, peppered with learned quotations from Raymond Williams and Northrop Frye, proved too much for several young Asians in the audience, who staged a noisy walk-out. One of those who remained, a young woman, expressed the outrage all of them obviously felt when she jumped up and said, 'There is something wrong when a book of this kind is called literature.' The floor was not polarised – as it tended to be in the London television studios – along racial or religious lines. A number of middle-aged whites in the audience supported the Muslim view that it was outrageous to call Rushdie's filth 'literature'. One woman in a noisy cotton dress stated that the rot and begun with the trial of Lady Chatterley. Since then the tide of filth and obscenity reaching the bookstores had become overwhelming. What was wanted was a return to the decent Christian values the Muslims were the only people brave enough to stand up for.

Anwar was the most vociferous of those defending the Muslim position: He kept jumping up indignantly and repeating, in a voice as plain as Yorkshire pudding, 'The book is offensive:

you have to take that as the starting line. You won't acknowledge the offence. We are unhappy that you won't acknowledge
the offence.'

There was something in Anwar's manner that radiated
honesty: there seemed no way he could be part of a wider
conspiracy of protest engineered by the Maududists or any
other Islamic faction. He had obviously thought out his position
by himself. I buttonholed him after the meeting, and within
minutes he had invited me back to his house.

His home, a back-to-back not far from the college, was spot-
lessly clean. His wife Leila – decently clad in a brown headscarf
– served us curried vegetables and samozas, while two young
children played on the floor. After the meal we repaired upstairs
to a small narrow study, so Leila could feed her children.

Anwar taught biology at a local, mainly Asian, secondary
school. Born in Lahore, he had arrived in Britain at the age of
eight. His father had migrated a few years earlier. For most of
the time he worked in the mills as an electrician. Like most
of the Pakistanis of his generation, his father had expected to
return; but soon he realised that he wasn't going to become a
millionaire after working in a mill for a few years. He stayed
and survived, but did not prosper; and, deciding to make the
best of things, brought over his family.

For Anwar the excitement of the move was quickly dispelled
by his astonishment at being in England. He and his father had
expected Britain to be a beautiful green place of lush meadows
and running streams, not unlike the Islamic vision of paradise.
Instead they found it a land of perpetual winter, a world
enclosed by cloud. Anwar could hardly believe this was the
same planet – or that the grey-skinned natives, perpetually
garbed in big boots and thick overcoats, belonged to the same
human race. Still, being a bright boy, he got on well at school.
He could already read and write some English when he arrived,
in addition to Urdu and Punjabi, his mother tongue. The special
classes in English at his secondary school enabled him to catch
up; but they also kept him socially apart from the whites.

It was his father who had instructed him in the Qur'an. The
emphasis was on learning to read and recite it in Arabic in order
to be able to follow those parts of it that came in the prayers. It

was not till later, when Anwar went to university, that he learned the meanings in English. Anwar was not aware of his father's religious affiliation: he professed not to know about the difference between the various subcontinental sects – the Deobandis, the Barelwis and the Jamaatis, the different Bradfordian *pirs*. His father had what Anwar thought was a simplistic view: you had to have religion, and you had to have the world. You had to satisfy both. As Anwar grew up and began to read the Qur'an for himself in English, he disagreed with his father. He saw religion and the world – *al din wa al dunya* – as one.

'There's no separation in Islam,' he told me. 'It's all just One. You can't be God-conscious some of the time and then unconscious.'

The remark was revealing, confirming the tendency noted by informed observers that a quantum change occurs in the religion of migrants moving from countryside to city, or from a Muslim to a European country. Werner Schiffauer, who has studied Turkish peasants in their home villages in Anatolia and in Germany, notes what he calls the 'islamisation of the self' among urban immigrants and migrants to Europe. In the village or homeland, religious practice is unreflecting, bound up with rhythms of peasant life. In the village society oscillates between two states, according to the rhythms dictated by the Islamic calendar: at secular times the village consists largely of autonomous households, in which relationships are based on the classic polarities of honour and shame and 'the reciprocal exchange of offerings and provocations'. During sacred times (the five daily prayers and congregational prayer on Fridays, the month of Ramadan, the holy nights and the *'id*s or religious festivals) the whole society 'changes into a religious community'. The Islamic rituals establish an alternative social structure which complements the secular one, in which brotherhood replaces opposition, in which one no longer protects one's honour against others but collectively honours God, in which sharing replaces exchange and so forth. Religious thought in the village takes the form of 'collective self-certainty', in which the legal norms, the do's and don'ts of Islam, are central: discussion focuses on such questions as 'whether the sin of eating pork is greater or less than that of drinking raki, or how one can accumulate the most religious merit'.[1] Abroad the Turkish Muslim no longer encounters the person with whom he has ties of reciprocity but a person of similar mind. 'During sacred times, society no longer changes into a religious community, but, rather, one leaves the society and enters the religious community.' The latter 'often becomes a counterweight to the secular society, as well as a place of retreat, a haven' where, in contrast to the outside society, 'one is treated with respect and esteem, a place where the value and dignity of individuals are recognised – as opposed to the external society where one often feels discriminated against and humiliated.'[2] The process is an aspect of a wider phenomenon, the privatising of religion. A person's social standing no longer depends on membership of the religious community.

This privatising of religion is an essential component of what is generally called 'fundamentalism'. Among Christians, those who experience this change talk of a private relationship with Jesus, whom they claim to have taken as their *personal* saviour. Among Muslims such as Anwar, the privatisation is more likely to take the form of internalising the text of the Qur'an by self-education. Though few 'born-again Muslims' would acknowledge it, the privatising of Islam – which, as Schiffauer points out, 'bespeaks a totally new concern with the self' – is a necessary state on the road to secularity.[3]

Anwar's use of the word 'God-conscious' – an essentially privatising formulation – was also significant. It alerted me to the fact that he had studied the Qur'an in Muhammad Asad's English translation, with its modernist *tafsir* or commentary. Asad – formerly Leopold Weiss, born in 1900 – is a convert from Judaism: a Viennese intellectual of the Koestler generation, his disillusionment with Western civilisation drew him not to the Communist 'god that failed', but to a romantic vision of Islam inspired by his admiration for King Abdul Aziz ibn Sau'd, the founder of Saudi Arabia, whose campaigns in the 1920s Weiss had covered for the *Frankfurter Allgemeiner Zeitung*. His mastery of Arabic, particularly in its Hejaz dialect, combined with his European background, enabled him to produce a version of the Qur'an in an English admirably suited to the needs of a modernising, privatised, anglophone Islam. Though highly regarded by progressive Muslims like Sheikh Yamani, the former Saudi oil minister, Asad's translation and commentary had fallen foul of the narrow strictures of the Saudi religious establishment and the Maududists who controlled the World Islamic League in Mecca. When I interviewed him in Tangier in 1980, Asad had become rather disillusioned by the state into which the Islamic world had fallen. He was incensed by Khomeini, whom he regarded as an 'ignorant mullah'. I asked him if, given a re-run of his life, he would take the road to Mecca again. He paused for what seemed a significantly long time: 'I haven't lost my faith' was all he would say.

Guided by Asad's *tafsir*, which dwells on the scientific and rationalistic elements in the text, Anwar found no conflict between revealed and scientific truth: 'If there were,' he said, 'it would challenge my faith.' Muslims did not have the same problems that Christian fundamentalists had: the Qur'an, unlike the Old Testament, was perfect and uncorrupted by human editing.

'Isn't there a conflict between the Qur'anic view of creation and Darwinian evolution?'

'Where's the conflict? The Qur'an teaches that God created Adam from dust. Every day I find myself teaching the children that living and non-living are being recycled all the time. Your and my bodies are constituted from nutrients which are from clay. God doesn't have to write the formula down – mineral composition and all that. He just says "clay". He's addressing human beings in language they can understand. It isn't a problem. Maybe Darwinianism was originally hostile to religion. Justifiably so, because religion was stultified. Judaeo-Christianity was telling people to believe in things they were seeing to be not true. Asking them to believe the earth was flat. We didn't have that problem in Islam, ever.'

I didn't trouble him with Sheikh Bin Baz, the chief mufti of Saudi Arabia, who annoyed the late King Feisal by publishing an article insisting that the Qur'an – the final word of God – teaches that the sun goes round the earth and that only infidels taught otherwise. I was in Bradford to listen.

For Anwar the beauty of the Qur'an – read through Muhammad Asad's modernist prism – was its celebration of reason.

'Contrary to what I may have expected, I found it very very logical and very very beautiful. That came as a surprise, because of the Islam I learned from my father. He had relied mainly on habit. What I worked out for myself was much more exciting.'

Was it not difficult to live the Muslim life at university?

'Not really. There were so many new experiences. But there was a difference between my exterior and my interior life. In my interior life I was drawn to Islam as to a magnetic pole. It made me feel a lot more content; it made me feel I had a better sense of reality than other people. Other people around me didn't seem to have progressed beyond the very superficial questions. I was surprised they were content with so little.'

After graduating in 1979 he went to Pakistan for a year, to stay with relatives. The country did not match his expectations. Though he enjoyed himself travelling around, he was disappointed in his relatives, and they – he sensed – may have been disappointed in him. They expected him to be more Westernised, more secular in outlook; he found them rather frivolous and materialistic, somewhat naïve in their enthusiasm for everything Western. Relative to his family in England they had travelled faster: by Pakistani standards they had become quite rich.

Not that the poor were necessarily more religious in the true sense, though they were more observant. The religion was not understood spiritually. The few people whom he met who had opened the door to it were very enlightened and knowledgeable, much more self-confident than other people. They had a stronger sense of their own identities as Pakistanis.

On returning to England Anwar did his teacher training. He spent a lot of time reading about Islam. He studied the works of Maududi, whose systematic and logical approach he found appealing, although as he became more familiar with Islam he became more critical. He never entertained the idea of joining the Jamaat.

'They can show us the way,' he said, 'but they can't solve our problems. They can't tell us how to do it. We're in a better position to judge our situation than they are.'

It was an item on local radio that first alerted him to *The*

Satanic Verses; then he encountered the quotations circulated by the Jamaat-i-Islami in the mosque.

'Most people would say these passages were taken out of context,' he said. 'I can't see what context could possibly justify such language.'

'What you're really saying is that words have a power beyond context?' I said.

'No. I'm saying that certain words have a certain plain meaning.' This sounded very Yorkshire. 'To try to justify them in terms of context or in a literary manner just doesn't appeal to me. I just don't accept it.'

'You wouldn't accept that if someone has a bad dream with forbidden things it would be OK to write it down?'

'I believe that everything that I say, or I do, or I write has an effect, whether I'm aware of it or not. We're responsible. We can't always say how we feel.'

I repeated the argument about context, pointing out that the sequences Muslims found so objectionable happened in dreams to a character suffering a psychotic breakdown. The language might be offensive, but surely Rushdie had set things up in such a way as to make it quite clear there was no authorial endorsement?

'The argument doesn't wash,' said Anwar. 'Supposing Punch exposes himself in front of the children, the man in the booth who pulls all the strings cannot say, "It's not me, it's the puppet!" Everything in that show is created by the puppeteer – the man who wrote the novel. It might be a very clever way of saying how he feels. I know that if I want to say something to somebody sometimes which I think might offend them I might say: "So-and-so said this about you, how do you react to that?" That would be my way of getting the message across and gauging his reaction at the same time while avoiding the blame. In any case, he has used historical characters: he's talked about the Prophet, about the Angel Gabriel, the Messenger's messenger, who is a very holy figure for Muslims, a very significant being in the Islamic cosmos. After all, if Gabriel's not a true messenger, then the Message cannot be true. Any twisting or any distortion of this character is going to be seen as an attempt to falsify the scriptures.'

'It doesn't falsify them at all,' I said. 'The scriptures are there. If the scriptures are true they will withstand any manner of attack.'

'Yes, the scriptures are there, but not everybody reads them. Most people in the West haven't read the Qur'an. They hadn't even heard of Gibreel till they read this book. This is their first impression of his character. There are truths here which people haven't discovered or haven't decided on, and here's this man already presenting them in a distorted form. I think he's not doing those people a great service. He's offending people we hold dear; and it's also a great loss to those people who haven't yet discovered our scripture.'

'But you've studied Islam and know that what's in the book isn't true. Why does it matter, since you know the truth?'

'Because it offends me that lies should be propagated. I am a Muslim and for me Islam stands for the propagation of truth. It offends me that someone should be allowed not just to propagate an alternative version of the truth, but actually to distort the truth.'

'Yes, but fiction is fiction: it does not pretend to be truth.'

'But the image has been conveyed: once you've said something it's conveyed. If you read something fictitious in a pornographic magazine, the picture it conveys may not be true. But the image stays with you. It's when your daughter comes up to you that the idea comes home that perhaps Page Three really is offensive to women. The image has an impact. So does the word. Once the word is uttered, it's uttered. You cannot unsay it. You cannot justify it by saying "it was only a joke!" The fact is that these things affect people. That's the trouble with his title, *The Satanic Verses*. It's highly provocative. People will assume that it applies to the whole of the Qur'an.'

'It comes in Tabari . . .'

'Yes, but the lives of the Prophet aren't canonical. The story has no authentic basis. There's nothing in the text that could authenticate that story. The Muslim historians when they were collecting materials put in everything: they left the decision to exclude or include things to their successors. They didn't see it as their duty to evaluate the quality of the reports. That came afterwards, with the collectors of the *hadiths*, like al-Bukhari and Muslim. The *hadith*-collectors went over all the stories with a toothcomb, and checked both their content and origins very carefully. The story of the Satanic Verses isn't in any of the major *hadith* collections. To imply that even one verse of the Qur'an could have been inspired by the devil undermines all of the rest. If a single word can be proved to be of other than divine origin, the Qur'an is not the Qur'an – it is not what it says it is, the utterance of God.'

'It could still be ninety-nine per cent true . . .'

'No, no. It has to be one hundred per cent. Muhammad challenged his critics to produce a single *sura* [chapter] like the Qur'an, and they couldn't. The Qur'an guarantees itself – if this is the Book of God and God Himself says "I will protect it", and he turns out not to have done so then this isn't the Book of God.'

His certainty was absolute, as if he were stating a scientific fact. To his scientific mind the Qur'an was an instrument of high technology – like a spacecraft or a supersonic airliner. The smallest design fault, a defective screw or leaking fuel-seal, would bring his faith crashing to earth in flames.

'But what,' I said, 'if someone were to produce evidence that it wasn't what it purported to be, that it was really a collection of oral utterances and traditions collected a century or more after the Prophet's death, would that damage your faith?'

'Well, I'd want to see the evidence: if you doubt, "produce one *sura* like it".[4] Show where this comes from, show who put it together! Where can you find one book that says everything about everything?'

'There are other holy books . . .'

'Where? Show them to me!'

'It's a question of how you read the text. Religious believers read their sacred texts in a special way. Christian fundamentalists believe the Bible to be without error; Mormons think their holy book, the Book of Mormon, is a flawless text preserved on golden tablets, which describes how Jesus converted the pre-Columbian Americans to Christianity. Lots of people think their holy books contain all the truth that there is to know. Of course there are truths buried in ancient texts: they contain the accumulated wisdom of many generations. But it's absurd to claim that these texts have been handed down without human editing. Even if you accept the idea of revelation, God reveals himself through human language – in the case of the Qur'an, the language He chose was Arabic. Are you trying to tell me He didn't use phrases or expressions that already existed in that language? If that was the case, why did the early Arab grammarians rely so heavily on pre-Islamic poetry to discover the rules of grammar that would make it possible for them to understand the Qur'an? It's not that I'm doubting the many truths in the Qur'an, it's your insistence on one hundred per cent. I don't see that it matters if some sections of text are thought to be interpolations.'

'It matters because the text has to live up to the criteria it establishes for itself. The text has gone out of its way to tell you "I am beyond corruption." If a single word has been added or subtracted, the whole edifice collapses!'

'But the Qur'an was originally delivered orally. It was only after Muhammad had spoken that his utterances were written down on things like camel bones and palm leaves.'

'What difference does that make?'

'When you use the word "text" it implies the finished product, whereas at the time that the various passages that make up the Qur'an are supposed to have been revealed the textual edifice was incomplete: how can you possibly talk of one hundred per cent certainty about the authenticity of a text which consists of a compilation of oral utterances?'

'The one thing Muslims can be one hundred per cent certain of is that the Qur'anic text has been preserved in its perfection. Even non-Muslim writers confirm that it is the most perfect book in the world. There is no other book that has stood for fourteen centuries unaltered. Whether it comes from God or not, the one thing everyone, Muslim or non-Muslim, can be certain of is that the Book consists of what Muhammad said. The fact that there are oral traditions doesn't mean that they were interpolations. Muhammad's Companions and the professional Reciters memorised the text. Then, when a large number of them were killed in battle, and it was feared that the remainder would soon die, the words were written down . . .'

There I left it. I had broken my rule, had become involved in argument. But the argument had been instructive. Anwar the natural scientist had a naïve, unscientific view of what was essentially a literary question. Just as most of the Biblical inerrantists I had met in America – other than religious professionals like preachers or theologians – had been physicians, chemists, computer specialists, or engineers, people whose understanding of reality was rooted in the factualistic realm of applied science and technology, so Anwar, the most articulate of the fundamentalists I met in Bradford (given that Shabbir Akhtar wasn't really a fundamentalist at all, at least not according to any recognised definition) had been a teacher of biology, a man whose understanding of texts – a 'textbook' understanding – came largely from manuals devoted to specific branches of science. Social surveys confirm that it is much more rare for fundamentalists to belong to professions such as law, where the use of language is value-oriented.[5] For all the jeremiads that fundamentalism, Islamic and Christian, lances at Western 'materialism', it is fundamentalism that is hard, factualistic and philistine, impervious to the multi-layered nuances of meaning that reside in texts, in fictions, in music and iconographies, in the cells of art and culture where modernity – that universal modernity created by a vibrant, still dynamic 'West' – stores its spiritual wealth. It is mostly those who are already spiritually impoverished, those who are too ill-educated or culturally isolated to enjoy the fruits of Western culture who fulminate against Western 'godlessness', unable to discern the divine both in nature and art. Fundamentalism is the most materialistic of contemporary ideologies, a throwback to the mechanistic values of the Victorians. It thrives among the deracinated, who compensate for physical displacement by seeking impious certainties in language.

The very richness of the Qur'an as a text was traduced by Anwar's insistence on 'one hundred per cent'. For the strongest, most mind-expanding message that emerges from that extraordinary collection of inspired utterances – whether they are the utterances of one man or, as some scholars think, the recycled distillation of generations – warns against the sin of *shirk*, or associating other beings with God. Yet Sunni Islam, lacking an educated priesthood, seemed to have committed that very sin, elevating God's Book into a kind of fetish, an object of idolatrous veneration.

Due to a combination of political weakness and populist pressure the Caliphate had surrendered its intellectual leadership as far back as the ninth century, initiating that long decline in a movement that once seemed to have heralded a brilliant future for the whole of the human race. The enlightened traditions of Islam had to be hidden against populist bigotry behind the esoteric discourse fostered by schismatic sectarians such as the Brethren of Purity. As early as the tenth or eleventh century, the latter, a group of philosophers based at Basra in Iraq, perceived the Qur'an, not as a book of answers, but of questions. Its depictions of paradise, where the virtuous spent their time deflowering virgins, and hell, where the wicked suffered eternal fire, were intended, they insisted, only for the ignorant who could not be induced to seek the one and shun the other unless they could be described in terms they could comprehend. For the Brethren, heaven and hell were essentially states of mind: hell consisted of the dull, sublunary world of 'generation and corruption' – a world, one might hazard, filled with obsessions about *izzat* or family honour, about the proper place and headgear for women, about meticulous observance of pharisaic rules; heaven was the 'abode of spirits in the vast expanse of the universe' – the cosmic dimensions available to the human imagination. These enlightened men had no doubt that the kind of fetishism that interpreted the Qur'an exoterically, instead of searching out its inner meanings, was the essence of 'disbelief (*kufr*), error, ignorance and blindness'.[6]

Textual fetishism, the crime the letter commits against the spirit, is not confined to one-dimensional interpretation; the sin also resides in a dogged and arrogant refusal to recognise the oral implications of the text:

Seen from outside [the Qur'an] appears . . . to be a collection of sayings and stories that is more or less incoherent and at first approach in places incomprehensible; the reader who is not forewarned, whether he reads the text in translation or in Arabic, runs up against obscurities, repetitions, tautologies and, in most of the long *suras*, a certain dryness without

having at least the 'sensory consolation' of that beauty of
sound which emerges from ritual and correctly intoned reading. But such difficulties are to be met in one degree or
another in most sacred scriptures. The seeming incoherence
of these texts – for instance the Song of Songs or certain
passages of the Pauline Epistles – always has the same cause,
the incommensurable disproportion between the Spirit and
the limited resources of human language.[7]

There is a much more prosaic explanation for the seeming
incoherence noted by Frithjof Schuon, a prominent Western
convert to Sufism. The Qur'an, like most other sacred texts,
occurs at the historic juncture between orality and literacy. This
radically affects both its status and the way it is understood.
Indeed, it would hardly be too strong to say that the cult of the
text, of which Sunni Islam is an outstanding example, is the
characteristic posture of a society moving away from pure orality
into the realm of literacy, before the literate outlook has fully
taken hold.

From the perspective of scholarship, as distinct from piety,
the origins of the Qur'anic text are obscure. According to some
Muslim traditions, the Prophet's utterances were dictated by
him and first written down on whatever materials came to
hand, such as camel-bones, palm leaves, fragments of wood or
parchment. Others tell that Muhammad's followers learned the
whole of the Qur'an by heart, and that the text was only written
down when there appeared a danger that the memorisers were
being lost in battle. As Michael Cook observes, these 'traditions
are not a model of consistency'.[8] There is general agreement
that the final collection was made during the reign of the Caliph
'Uthman (644–56), who ordered all variant texts to be destroyed.
While it is certainly the case that variants in the text are negli-
gible in terms of content, archaeological and numismatic evidence suggests that in fact the canonised text was fixed
somewhat later.[9] The internal evidence is equally problematic.
The wealth of allusions in the Qur'an presuppose a familiarity
with Jewish and Christian scriptures, as well as with the events
of Muhammad's career: unlike, say, the synoptic Gospels, the
Qur'an is literally unintelligible without reference to sources

outside itself – references liberally supplied by the Qur'anic ex-
egetes from the *hadiths* and from the *sirat* or biographies of the
Prophet recorded by the early annalists. There are also marked
variations in style, ranging between the shorter more ecstatic
passages, presumed to date from the earlier, Meccan, period of
the Prophet's career, and the later Medinese *suras* when Muhammad the lawmaker was giving instructions to his community.
There are, however, some marked exceptions to this pattern.

Even more striking is the frequency with which alternative
versions of the same passage coexist in different parts of the
text. As Michael Cook observes, 'when placed side by side,
these versions often show the same sort of variation as one
finds between parallel versions of oral traditions'.[10] John Wansburgh, a leading scholar of Semitic languages, goes considerably
further than this: 'The Qur'an,' he says, 'is not the carefully
executed project of one or many men, but rather the product of
an organic development from originally independent traditions
during a long period of transmission.'[11]

What seems beyond doubt, and is recognised in Islamic
tradition, is that the Qur'an is a text constructed out of what
were originally oral materials, whether these are thought to be
the verbal utterances of Muhammad dictated to him by God,
or Wansburgh's 'originally independent traditions'. The idea of
the Prophet as a passive 'mouthpiece' or 'telephone' for God is
far from being unique to Islam, and exists in many oral cultures.
For example, the Delphic oracle was not responsible for her
oracular utterances, which were held to be the voice of the god;
in the neo-oral culture of the television age, the Delphic idea
has been revived by individuals (mostly female) known as
'channellers' who claim to speak on behalf of quasi-divine
'entities' from the outer reaches of space-time.[12]

The style of literature, including sagas and epics, originating
in orality, has certain general characteristics which readers of
the Qur'an would readily recognise. Since oral works lack page
numbers or indexes, they rely extensively on mnemonics for
information retrieval:

In a primary oral culture, to solve effectively the problem of
retaining and retrieving carefully articulated thought, you

have to do your thinking in mnemonic patterns, shaped for ready oral recurrence. Your thought must come into being in heavily rhythmic, balanced patterns, in repetitions or antitheses, in alliterations and assonances, in epithetic and other formulary expressions, in standard thematic settings . . . in proverbs which are constantly heard by everyone so that they come to mind readily and which themselves are patterned for retention and ready recall, or in other mnemonic form. Serious thought is intertwined with memory systems. Mnemonic needs determine even syntax.[13]

The seemingly chaotic organisation of the Qur'anic text which struck Carlyle and other literate Europeans as a 'wearisome, confused jumble, crude, incondite; endless iterations, long-windedness, entanglement . . . insupportable stupidity, in short!'[14] is no bar to mnemonic retrieval.[15] All good Muslims, including the Muslims of Bradford, are required to learn the Qur'an by heart in Arabic, reaffirming the primal orality of their culture.

Most cultures, of course, retain a lingering residue of orality, often for centuries after the invention of writing or even print. In semi-oral (or semi-literate) cultures, literacy tends to be the preserve of an elite, ensuring that orality remains the predominant thinking mode of the masses. This is especially the case where writing is difficult. Semitic alphabets, being the earliest to have appeared, are also the least developed. Only consonants are written, leaving the reader to supply the appropriate vowels. Readers of Arabic, Hebrew, Persian or Urdu – languages written in Semitic scripts – have to draw on data from outside the text: they have to know the language and its grammar in order to know which vowels to supply between the consonants.[16] This is why the invention of the easily learned Greek alphabet, in which vowels are written, was not only a technological revolution: it led to a democratisation of culture. The spread of Christianity from its original Jewish matrix was the direct consequence of the fact that the Gospels were written in Greek. The canonising of the text, first in Greek and later in Latin, represented a movement away from orality – a process greatly accelerated after the Reformation by the development of print.

Manuscript cultures, of course, are closer to orality than cultures where print has taken over: those people who can read, often professionals, commonly continue to vocalise *sotto voce*, to memorise passages for easier retrieval.[17]

Arabic, like Hebrew, retains a closer connection with primary orality than European tongues. The Qur'an – unique among Islamic texts – is always printed with short vowel signs to ensure that when read aloud, as it must be for liturgical purposes, it is read correctly. The correct oral articulation is an essential aspect of its divine significance: the very first word addressed to the Prophet by the Archangel Gabriel – *Iqra!* – means both 'read' and 'recite'. The two opposing directions of transmission, the difference as it were, between input and output, are not distinguished from each other. The same deep connection with orality is maintained in Islamic law, where oral testimony still predominates and written affidavits are not usually taken in evidence.

Walter Ong argues convincingly that the shift from orality to literacy has had the profoundest imaginable effect on human culture and psychology – more profound, perhaps, than any other industrial or technological change of which we are aware. The very notion of history is a product of literacy, as is the idea of literature: 'thinking of oral genres as oral literature is like thinking of horses as automobiles without wheels.'[18] For the pre-literate, as Malinowski noted, language is a mode of action, not a countersign of thought. The word in its 'natural, oral habitat' is part of an existential present. Spoken words always reach out beyond themselves: they do not occur alone, in isolation.[19] 'Sight isolates, sound incorporates. Whereas sight situates the observer outside what he views, at a distance, sound pours into the hearer . . . I am at the centre of my auditory world which envelops me, establishing me at a kind of core sensation and existence.'[20] Whereas the visual media of writing and print tend to isolate, the oral word retains its power. These differences are so profound that they radically affect the way people behave under conditions of extreme stress or tension: 'orals commonly exteriorise schizoid behaviour, where literates interiorise it' – in effect, whereas the literates classicly withdraw schizophrenically into dream worlds of their own, 'oral folk commonly manifest their schizoid tendencies by extreme external confusion' – for example, by 'going berserk'.[21]

According to Ong, the interiorising force of the oral word relates in a special way to the sacral, to the 'ultimate concerns of existence'. This is why in 'most religions the spoken word functions integrally in ceremonial and devotional life'.[22] Cultures retaining a substantial oral residue remain 'word-attentive' in a way that is absent in the typographical universe. Buying something in a Middle Eastern bazaar is not a simple commercial transaction: it is a 'series of verbal and somatic manoeuvres, a polite duel, a contest of wits, an operation in oral agonistic'.[23] One might add that the same applies *a fortiori* to blasphemies, expletives or insults: oral utterances or written versions thereof that literates would tend to regard as innocuous badinage or word-play, mimicking the crudities of street language, may, for orals, be understood quite differently:

> The fact that oral peoples commonly and in all likelihood universally consider words to have magical potency is clearly tied in, at least unconsciously, with their sense of the word as necessarily spoken, sounded and hence power-driven. Deeply typographic folk forget to think of words as primarily oral, as events, and hence as necessarily powered: for them, words tend rather to be assimilated to things, 'out there' on a flat surface. Such 'things' are not so readily associated with magic, for they are not actions, but are in a radical sense dead, though subject to dynamic resurrection.[24]

The oral–typographic distance is particularly apposite in discussing the forms of literature. Whereas most types of poetry, or for that matter 'divine recitation' such as the Qur'an, belong firmly at the oral end of the literary spectrum, the novel is 'clearly a print genre, deeply interior, de-heroicised and tending strongly to irony'.[25] This applies particularly to the postmodernist novel, where stories are de-plotted and characters 'hollowed out' to represent extreme states of consciousness, as in Kafka, Beckett, Pynchon[26] – and, of course, Salman Rushdie.

Was it Rushdie's error to have resurrected those 'dead' words, converting his clever literary fireworks into lethal missiles?

What would make such a conclusion doubly ironic is the use he makes of oral traditions within the post-modernist genre he espouses. He excels in the role of fabulist, drawing on the whole range of Eastern story-telling to fill his 'hollowed out' characters with narratives. It is true, no doubt, that his words – the words of a highly sophisticated, post-modernist conjuror, designed for 'deeply typographic folk' – were yanked by others from their matrix in the typographical universe and transplanted to the mental world of the North-West Frontier. That this should have happened is not at all surprising in the age of the photo-copier and the fax machine, and with a writer as well-known in his native land as Salman Rushdie.

Conclusion

On 21 October 1989, on the occasion of the Prophet Muhammad's birthday, a prominent supporter of the Iranian revolution in Britain, Dr Kalim Siddiqui, addressed a gathering of five hundred Muslims in Manchester. The meeting was attended by Gerald Kaufman, the Labour Party's spokesman on foreign affairs, as well as the Bishop of Manchester. In his speech Dr Siddiqui said: 'The Muslim community has overwhelmingly endorsed the death sentence passed on Rushdie by the late Imam Khomeini. That *fatwa* which is according to the divine law of Islam will remain valid until executed . . .' He added that every time a Muslim saw a copy of *The Satanic Verses* displayed in a bookshop or library 'he feels personally insulted and humiliated. He is also reminded of his duty to bring to book those guilty of this capital offence against Islam.' Dr Siddiqui asked those who supported the Ayatollah Khomeini's *fatwa* to raise their hands. The vast majority did so. The action was caught by the television cameras, and reported in the press.

In the outrage that followed several voices were raised demanding that Dr Siddiqui be prosecuted for incitement to murder. The *Sun* urged the government to tell Siddiqui 'to pack up and go, preferably to Iran'. The *Independent* also demanded that Siddiqui be prosecuted for overstepping the boundaries of freedom of speech. The Home Office Minister, John Patten, condemned Siddiqui's statement as wholly irresponsible: 'peaceful protest was one thing, statements like this are truly unacceptable.'[1]

Unacceptably or otherwise, Dr Siddiqui enjoyed considerable

support among sections of the Muslim community in Britain. In mid-December, as this book went to press, he helped organise a Day of Muslim Solidarity in which the *imams* of a number of British mosques were urged to support the *fatwa* in their Friday sermons. Although reports that 1,000 mosques took part in the Day of Muslim Solidarity appeared to be wildly exaggerated,[2] it was nevertheless clear that the anti-Rushdie campaign was maintaining its momentum. An opinion poll conducted among British Muslims by the BBC in October had reported strong support for the suppression of *The Satanic Verses* and 'significant approval' for the *fatwa*.[3] By the end of 1989 an impasse appeared to have been reached: *The Satanic Verses* remained on the shelves of Britain's bookshops; Rushdie's life continued to be in serious danger; Penguin executives, torn between their contractual obligations to Salman Rushdie and concern for the safety of their staff, continued to postpone the paperback version. Meanwhile the mantle of protest had passed to the Iranians and their representatives, now that the Saudi-backed Jamaatis, who did so much to promote the agitation in its initial stage, had backed out of the picture. Dr Siddiqui had been notably silent when the book first came out, before Khomeini's *fatwa*. A year after publication the book was still a 'political football' between rival Muslim factions in a wider campaign for the allegiance of Muslims in Britain and elsewhere.

Khomeini's *fatwa* was an act of political opportunism engineered by factions inside Iran for local political reasons: the fact that it was issued two months after the book had been reviewed in Tehran makes this abundantly clear. The agitation had started in India and Pakistan. The Jamaat-i-Islami were in near the beginning: Jamaatis alerted their colleagues in Britain and drafted the statements that were issued by both the Central London Mosque and the South African government. They milked the issue for all it was worth, but they did not necessarily start the agitation. This appears to have originated in India, more or less spontaneously, in response to Rushdie's interviews: given the sensitivities over the Babri Masjid, the Shah Banu case and the rioting in Bangalore over *Muhammad the Idiot*, the furore in India was an absolute certainty. Even without the prospect of a general election in November 1989, communal tensions were running higher than at any time since Independence.

Once the Jamaat became involved it was inevitable that sooner or later the Iranians would respond: the Jamaatis enjoy close links with the Saudi Arabian Wahhabis, historical enemies of the Shi'a. For the Ayatollah to have stood idly by after the Islamabad shootings would have meant ceding his claim to the global leadership of Islam. The fuel for the agitation, both in Britain and abroad, was the Saudi–Iranian rivalry. In pronouncing *fatwa* – and in effectively calling for its implementation – both the Ayatollah and Dr Siddiqui were *ultra vires*, acting outside their competence. Under no Islamic rubric can the Britain in which Salman Rushdie wrote and published his book be considered part of *Dar al Islam* where Islamic courts are supposed to, but rarely have, jurisdiction. Moreover, in pronouncing sentence without trial, the Ayatollah was preempting its outcome: as several of the Iranian leader's Muslim critics pointed out, the question of whether or not *The Satanic Verses* was blasphemous, and whether its author should be judged an apostate, must be decided in a properly constituted *Shari'a* court of law.

This point, however, should not be allowed to obscure the fact that if Rushdie had published his book in Egypt or Pakistan, he could quite legitimately have been condemned to death according to the laws of Islam. Would public opinion in the West, unanimously outraged by the *fatwa*, have acknowledged the right of an Islamic tribunal to condemn Rushdie? The question is not entirely hypothetical, given that the guru of the Egyptian fundamentalists, Sheikh Umar Abdul Rahman, has pronounced a similar ruling on the Nobel prizewinning novelist Neguib Mahfouz. It speaks well for the Egyptian state that it was the Sheikh, not the novelist, who found himself in prison.

In this respect it is instructive to recall the words of Ibn Taymiyya and other Islamic legal authorities: insulting the Prophet is an offence against God, punishable by death. The only question to be determined by a *Shari'a* court, apart from proving that the offence has taken place, is to decide whether the culprit should be spared if he repents.

Quite apart from the problems it raises for freedom of speech, the Rushdie Affair has drawn attention to, and thrown into relief, one of Islam's central problems: as well as being a system of belief and divine mythology, Islam is a system of law. To abandon that law is to acknowledge that Islam's most central institution – its Church, as it were – is defunct. Ever since the eighteenth century, when the Islamic world came under European control, Muslims have tried to grapple with the problem of legal reform: none of the attempts to harmonise Islamic systems with imported European ones has been successful. The most drastic solution – adopted by Turkey – may yet prove to have been the most successful: complete abolition of the *Shari'a*. (Yet even secular Turkey, like all Muslim countries, has banned Rushdie's book under populist pressure.) Where the *Shari'a* survives, the rule of law in its Western sense, essential to democratic government, is constantly in danger of being subverted by the challenge of Islamic legalism. 'Give us back the *Shari'a*,' say the Islamic activists, 'and all will be well.' The Rushdie Affair dramatises the implications of that demand. Should the Muslim governments yield to it, intellectual freedom and creativity, vital for social and economic success in today's global culture, would be smothered, just as it was gradually extinguished after the defeat of the Mu'tazilis by the forces of populism eleven centuries ago.

Despite its dramatic decline as a world civilisation, Islam is still 'programmed for victory'. Yet Muslims are still, a millennium and a half after their historic triumph, a global minority and, culturally speaking, a minority in their own societies, given Islam's attachment to cultural hegemony, its insistence that every aspect of human life be proved by revelation from God. The law in which so much Muslim energy has been invested over the centuries makes practically no provisions for Muslims as a minority. Its formation derives from the centuries after the Arab conquest, when the new faith was in its most triumphalist phase. Islamic tolerance towards the *dhimmis*, the subject peoples of the empire, reflects the magnanimity of conquest: it is the material counterpart of the Merciful Deity whose compassion is contingent on good behaviour. It is not a charter of rights for the conquered in any modern understanding of the term.

The assumption of dominance proceeds from a theology of

power which rests uneasily in psyches facing the reality of powerlessness. The rage of Islam which features so much in the world's headlines today is not so much Marx's 'cry of the oppressed' as the anguish of frustration.

To state the problem in these stark terms is to challenge the wisdom of those Christian and other voices, including influential voices in the Labour Party, that have been raised in defence of the 'outraged feelings' of Muslims. Since the eighteenth century Christian governments have gradually renounced the power of the state to protect Christian sensibilities. The blasphemy laws that remain part of the common law of England are vestigial relics, reflecting a long and honourable retreat from attempts to coerce the human mind in matters of faith. These laws are inequitable not only because they fail to protect non-Christians; they also fail to protect non-believers, based as they are on the premise that 'the religious sentiment offended deserves greater protection than that whose expression is inhibited.'[4] The militant atheist deserves the same right of free expression as the believing bigot: to state that polemics about religion should necessarily be expressed in polite language merely begs the question 'What is polite language?'

Unfortunately Britain, with its privileged state church and attachment to antique institutions, has been much less forthright in the defence of freedom than America, where any attempt to act on blasphemy laws would almost certainly fall foul of the constitutional separation of church and state. Yet, paradoxically, the United States is a far more religiously observant country than the United Kingdom. The American example should cause those people who argue that the blasphemy laws should be *extended* to protect Muslims and other non-Christian religions to think again: the American religious experience proves the opposite. Religion flourishes best when released from the umbrella of the state. What is needed is not improved protection of religion, but improved protection of freedom of speech.

Muslim activists were quite correct in pointing to the double standards prevailing in Britain: a government which tried to silence Peter Wright and which has muzzled broadcasters by

banning a political party, Sinn Fein, from appearing on radio
and television is not the most convincing advocate of Salman
Rushdie's right to publish. In a more genuinely pluralistic
culture British Muslims might well have felt less put upon by
Rushdie's book. As it is, the affair reveals a real grievance: as
it stands, the law of blasphemy discriminates against non-
Christians, as it discriminates against atheists. The law must be
abolished.

If the blasphemy laws were abolished verbal attacks on the
Islamic and other non-Christian religions could still be prosecuted under the Public Order Act, the Race Relations Act or
the various laws regulating 'defamatory' publications likely to
cause a 'breach of the peace': there are analogies in Northern
Ireland where sectarian provocations are banned by law. In a
free society limits of freedom of speech must be justified by the
possibility of harm inflicted to others: that is why there are libel
laws and why it is illegal to shout 'Fire!' in a crowded cinema.[5]
The problem with verbal attacks, of course, is that the notion
of harm is likely to be a subjective one. It will be understood in
different ways in different cultural contexts: in some societies,
publicly to cast doubt on the legitimacy of a person's birth while
suggesting that he regularly has sexual intercourse with his
mother will be deemed a heinous insult deserving of death; in
others, 'you motherfucking bastard' will be perceived as a
term of endearment. Intentions are crucial: not the least of the
objections to the present blasphemy laws is that they do not
take intentions into account. In theory, however, it should be
possible to draw a line between sectarian insults to persons
similar to the racial abuse forbidden under the Race Relations
Act, and the use of religious imagery for serious or artistic
purposes. A comparable distinction already exists with regard
to obscenity. It would be absolutely wrong to make religious
symbols into intellectual or artistic 'no go areas' in order to
protect the sensibilities of believers: as Charles Taylor observes,
there is 'something uniquely powerful about religious language
and symbols which makes even those who reject them need
them in order to explore their own universe.'[6]

Abolition or amendment of the law of blasphemy, however,
would scarcely touch on the complexity of the issues raised by

the Rushdie Affair. In one respect the whole campaign has been a disaster. Whatever claims they make to be 'defending the honour of Islam' the anti-Rushdie campaigners have seriously damaged the interests of Muslims in Britain. As R. W. Johnson points out in a perceptive article, the affair has eroded support for Muslim immigrants on the part of the left, the traditional ally of the disadvantaged, not only in Britain, but throughout Western Europe. 'In most of Europe now,' he concludes, 'if the right attacks the huddled forces of immigrant Islam, the left will mount, at best, a half-hearted, ambivalent defence.'[7] In France racism has increased substantially, with 46 per cent of people polled in a recent survey favouring repatriation of immigrants. The situation remains more ambiguous in Britain where, despite the prevalence of racism, immigrants are generally accorded more civil rights than their counterparts in France or Germany. But there can be no doubt that the publication of the book, followed by the Ayatollah's *fatwa* against its author, combined to produce a major setback to community relations in Britain. All over the country community leaders and other concerned people have expressed their dismay at what has taken place. Muslim youth, already alienated by the discrimination that exists in British society, has been driven down the separatist road. As a result of the grievance felt by Muslims of all ages, demands for voluntary aided Muslim schools have increased and will prove increasingly hard for the authorities to resist. The goal of social integration has become significantly more distant for a community whose thrift and industriousness had made it likely to prosper in the free market conditions created by Thatcherism.

Part of the responsibility for this state of affairs lies with the leadership of the Muslim community in Britain, particularly that of the Central London Mosque. In a situation that demanded caution and considerable sophistication, Dr al Ghamdi and his colleagues in the Union of Mosques Organisation and the Islamic Council of Europe simultaneously contrived to inflame Muslim opinion and to alienate important sections of the British public by their ill-informed and overheated response to Rushdie's book. Instead of explaining to the Muslim community that their decision to settle in Britain had placed them outside the 'protection' of *Dar al Islam* and the writ of the *Shari'a* law, they lent their authority to a campaign which they and their British advisors ought to have known would lead nowhere, since Rushdie had broken no British law. Given that the Islamic community is now an established part of the British population, the wisdom of allowing British Muslim institutions to be run by foreign-funded appointees possessing inadequate knowledge of British culture, law or institutions must be questioned.

Should we also blame Salman Rushdie for what has happened? Rushdie does not write his fiction in a political vacuum: both *Midnight's Children* and *Shame* are ironic attacks on the abuse of sacred mythologies in the service of power. He is not naïve in his views on political power: *The Jaguar Smile* displays a sophisticated grasp of political realities in developing societies.

Yet despite his knowledge of the Indian subcontinent and its Muslim cultures, he appears to have seriously misread the nature of the Islamic movements there and in other parts of the world. In this respect, however, he was far from being alone.

The revival of Islamic politics all over the world in the wake of the Iranian revolution of 1979 occasioned a vigorous debate among specialists about its meaning, tenor and long-term political implications. Put very crudely, the arguments crystallised round two broadly defined positions: the 'nominalists' and the 'essentialists'. Nominalists, who are generally on the left, try to explain the phenomenon in terms other than Islam itself: adapting the materialist, anti-idealistic perspectives of Marxism, they tend to see the various Islamic movements in the world as the product of social forces that can best be explained in terms of the secular categories of class or economic interest. Essentialists are more inclined to take an 'idealist' or phenomenological view, arguing that there is such a phenomenon as 'Islam' which, over the centuries, has undergone periods of cyclic revival. Nominalists are more likely than essentialists to claim that 'false consciousness' prevails among Muslim activists, and that demands for a restoration of Islamic law and government are being manipulated by powerful political or economic interests. Some of Rushdie's non-fictional writings, or non-fictional passages in his novels, suggest that in general he takes the nominalist view. In a passage from *Shame* already quoted he saw fundamentalism as something imposed by the Zia dictatorship: 'This is how religions shore up dictators; by encircling them with words of power, words which the people are reluctant to see discredited, disenfranchised, mocked.'

Similarly, in attacking Rajiv Gandhi Rushdie took the view that the ban on his book was part of the former Indian Prime Minister's wider 'misuse' of religion for political gain. He refused to address the threat of communal riots: 'I don't accept the public duty argument,' he told Roger Burford Mason. 'It seems to me that the job of the community leaders is to defuse these sentiments rather than exacerbate them. What's happening in India at the moment is that people pander to the worst things in Indian society and that makes them more and more powerful.'[8]

Rushdie, in this respect, might be characterised as 'secular fundamentalist'. He brooks no compromises with 'the worst things' represented by religious opposition to his book, either in India or in Britain where, at the time of writing, he has been actively pressing Penguin to issue the paperback version of *The Satanic Verses*, regardless of consequences. His views on religion are not universally shared within the international literary community: Wole Soyinka, the Nobel Prize-winning Nigerian writer, who has himself been in prison for opposing dictatorship, confessed in the summer of 1989 that 'given India's harrowing situation of religious unrest, I would probably have done the same if I were the Prime Minister'.[9]

The idea that religion is in itself an explosive force which has to be handled carefully because of its intrinsic psychical mobilising power is alien to the nominalist approach. For nominalists religion is 'false consciousness': indeed the 'true' interests of the people may require that the 'words of power' be neutralised by satire.

If this was indeed part of the intention behind *The Satanic Verses*, Rushdie may ultimately, of course, be vindicated. It is not improbable that the novel is enjoying a considerable 'underground' success among the elites in the Muslim world, those who have access to diplomatic passports and other privileges. Perhaps in the course of time the challenge it poses to Islamic mythologies will filter through the ideological prisms

imposed in various degrees by Muslim governments in deference to the power manipulated by the activists and the sentiments of the masses. However, this would be very much a
long-term scenario. In the short term, activist or fundamentalist
hands have been greatly strengthened by the furore over the
book's publication, particularly in the United Kingdom. Before
the Rushdie Affair few people took Dr Siddiqui seriously; now
he has a considerable following among British Muslims for
expressing the hard-line Khomeinist view.

It may also be argued that in *The Satanic Verses* Rushdie is a
novelist, not a propagandist. His novel is to Islam what *Portrait
of the Artist* is to Roman Catholicism: a form of spiritual auto-
biography, an exorcism of the repressive, punishing faith in
which he was brought up. He is charting the migrant's passage
from faith to disbelief through the minds of fictional characters;
moreover the passages which Muslims find most offensive, the
brothel scene in 'Return to Jahilia', occur in the dreams of a
fictional film star suffering a schizophrenic breakdown. It would
be naïve, however, to suppose that Rushdie could be protected
from the militant wrath of Muslims by the conventions of
fiction. Like other books for which large sums of money have
been paid, *The Satanic Verses* was massively 'hyped' by Salman
Rushdie and by Penguin, his publishers.

'One of the side effects of the mass media,' Umberto Eco
observed recently, 'is that they bring fiction to people who've
never read a novel before, and who don't share in the fictional
agreement, the suspension of disbelief.' There were probably,
he added, no more than 50,000 people in any country who
belonged to the category of novel-readers.[10]

It seems clear from the chronology of protest that Rushdie's
Muslim critics in India were alerted to the contents of *The·
Satanic Verses* even before the book became available, through
Rushdie's own pre-publication interviews. Like any author,
Rushdie sought the largest possible readership for his book.
The more he promoted it, however, the more its subversive
contents would come to the attention of people unequipped by
culture, education or inclination to read the work as fiction. As
the campaign progressed, it fully confirmed Eco's observation:
not only had the non- or recently-literate familiarised them-

selves with the offending passages, but even apparently sophisticated people like Shabbir Akhtar revealed a surprising lack of familiarity with the terms of the 'fictional agreement'. In condemning Rushdie's historical distortions he appeared to be unaware that those terms have long included the fictional treatment of historical personages.

'Literature is transactional,' remarks Gayatri Spivak. 'The point is not the correct description of a book, but the construction of readerships.'[11] In Rushdie's case the death of God/death of author symbolism represented by the 'guy upstairs' spills out, like so much else in this extraordinary novel, on to the street. Rushdie becomes the victim, writes Feroza Jussawalla, 'not so much of the Muslim's world as of indeterminacy, which is the condition of post-modernism, whereby authority has been completely wrested from the author and in his absence has been placed in the hands of warring factions of his readers.'[12]

It is the anti-Rushdie faction, of course, which has been the focus of this book. Among Western writers and readers, support for the beleaguered novelist has been nearly unanimous although politicians, who deal in a world where Rushdie's critics reside, have been more ambivalent. If the campaign against him originated in the Indian subcontinent, this is, to a large extent, where it remains to this day, given that parts of the subcontinent have been transplanted to Britain. Although Iranian representatives have tried to keep the issue alive in Europe, they have found little support among Muslim immigrants from Turkey and North Africa. The publication of *The Satanic Verses* in France and Germany passed with barely a squeak of protest. After the initial furore in the United States, when a number of bookstores were bombed or threatened with bombing, the issue went away, and the book lost its place on the bestseller lists.

In Britain, however, the campaign continues, without any resolution in sight. The primary reason, as I have tried to explain, is the treatment of the sacred personage of the Prophet. The protest has far more to do with honour than with faith.

The cult of Muhammad is deeply entrenched in the Muslim world, especially in the Indian subcontinent where few Muslims have access to the language of the Qur'an. The Prophet of Islam like other religious figures including Christ, may be a mythical construct. He is certainly a meta-historical one. But he is also a social fact. As such he is deeply ingrained in the collective psyche of the Muslim masses, including those who have recently settled in Britain. For the majority of Muslims, especially the masculine half, he has become an integral part of their identity. To deconstruct him using the symbols of medieval vilification is to play a very dangerous game indeed: about as dangerous as writing 'FUCK THE POPE' on the walls of the Catholic Falls Road in Belfast. We may agree with Rushdie's sentiments; we may salute his courage; we may admire his literary skill, without respecting his judgement.

As I argued earlier, Muslim identity in Britain is deeply bound up with the concept of honour, *izzat*, as practised in Indo-Pakistani village culture. The Prophet and his women are ideal types which evoke the sacred; even for the non-observant, who care little for theology, the 'honour of the Prophet' has meaning, as a focus for group allegiance and identity in a society where they suffer discrimination. The symbols are all the more potent because they reach into the region of *al ghaib* where the divine and the human, the sexual and the social are bonded: the sanctified figure of the Prophet, moreover, harks back to a more heroic age, when Muslims were in the ascendant.

The ayatollahs of the left, of course, may continue to insist that such concepts are mere reactionary opiates or masks that need to be removed before people will become aware of their true interests. The trouble is that what looks like a mask may actually be a shield: not so much a source of 'false consciousness' as a psychic protection against the real or perceived threat of annihilation. History often reveals that an attack on the mask will be interpreted as an attack on the person. Europeans paid dearly for the belief that fascism and Nazism could be 'unmasked' by merely informing the working class where their true interests lay. People do not always clearly distinguish between symbols and reality: Ulster Protestants whose 'true' interests might better be served in a united Ireland insist on worshipping in the Union Jack and the British monarchy the very symbols that make such a thing impossible. Ulster Catholics venerate the Pope, not for constitutional or theological reasons, but to enhance group loyalty in the face of perceived threats from loyalists.

Given Salman Rushdie's well-known commitment to community work and his record on race relations, the results of his book are savagely paradoxical. He is still in effect a prisoner in Britain – as much a hostage to the militant wrath of Islam as Roger Cooper in Tehran, and Brian Keenan, John McCarthy and Terry Waite in Lebanon, though his conditions are much less arduous: this is a scandal that cannot be rectified. Even if the Ayatollah, now dead, had chosen to revise his *fatwa* (an extremely unlikely event, whatever the diplomatic pressures) some zealot from Beirut, if not from Bradford, would have found another *faqih* to uphold the sentence. It can be of little comfort for Rushdie to know that the *fatwa* which deprived him of his freedom might have saved his life. I have been told in earnest by more than one Muslim resident in Britain that, had Rushdie not gone 'underground' for his own protection, a member of the community would have knifed him sooner or later. A sense of moral outrage that such things can happen in Britain takes us nowhere. In the electronic age, the quarrels of frontier villages erupt into people's living rooms every day.

Did Rushdie 'know what he was doing'? Is he a solitary crusader who is now having to suffer for his courage and noble intentions in taking on the dragons of bigotry? Is he a Muslim latter-day saint, a modern Hallaj who is now suffering a form of martyrdom for proclaiming the truth? Is he a more literary kind of martyr, a victim of 'indeterminacy', of leap-frogging technological change – a case, perhaps, of late *homo typographicus* stuck on the reefs of orality? Or is his a classic case of hubris, of the gifted artist who flies too near the sun of his own inspiration? It is much easier to take up positions defending the sacred rights of free speech, or the sacred person of a prophet, than to give a straight 'yes' or 'no' to these questions. Rushdie declined my invitation to talk on the telephone. That is his privilege. His number is ex-directory.

Sources

Note: *The Satanic Verses* (London, 1988) is cited as *TSV*

Prologue
1 Dante's *Inferno*, Canto xxviii, 22–7, tr. Dorothy L. Sayers. (Harmondsworth, 1969).
2 R. W. J. Austen, 'Islam and the Feminine', in Denis MacEoin and Ahmed al-Shahi (eds.), *Islam in the Modern World* (New York, 1983), p. 37.
3 Qur'an 4:34 (Arberry translation).
4 Muhammad Asad, *The Message of the Qur'an* (Gibraltar, 1980), p. 109, 110.
5 *ibid., loc. cit.*
6 See Edward Lane, *An Account of the Manners and Customs of the Modern Egyptians* (London, 1836: facsimile edn. New York, 1973), p. 82.
7 Qur'an, 4:25; Austen, *op. cit.*, p. 43.

Chapter 1:   Satanic Fictions
1 *Desert Island Discs*, BBC Radio 4, 8.9.88.
2 Timothy Brennan, *Salman Rushdie and the Third World: Myths of the Nation* (London, 1989), p. ix and *passim*.
3 *ibid.*, p. x.
4 *ibid.*, p. 101.
5 *ibid.*, p. 64.
6 See Salman Rushdie, *The Jaguar Smile* (London, 1987).
7 Brennan, *op. cit.*, p. 84.
8 *ibid.*, p. 102.
9 Feroza Jussawalla, *Family Quarrels: Towards a Criticism of*

Indian Writing in English (New York, 1985), p. 117; cited in Brennan, *op. cit.*, p. 109.

10 Salman Rushdie, *Midnight's Children* (New York and London, 1980), p. 420.

11 Salman Rushdie, *Shame* (New York and London, 1984), p. 251.

12 *India Today*, 15.8.88; quoted in Lisa Appignanesi and Sara Maitland, *The Rushdie File* (London, 1989), p. 39.

13 *Sunday*, India, 18–24.9.89.

14 *New Yorker*, 15.5.89, p. 127.

15 *TSV*, pp. 16–17.

16 Feroza Jussawalla, 'Resurrecting the Prophet: The Case of Salman, the Otherwise', in *Public Culture*, Vol. 2, No. 1, Fall 1989, p. 107.

17 *Midnight's Children*, p. 467; Brennan, *op. cit.*, p. 88.

18 Brennan, *op. cit.*, p. 153.

19 *TSV*, p. 4. There may be borrowings here from David Lodge's novel *Changing Places*: Lodge calls his mythical San Francisco Esseph; while one of his air-borne protagonists fantasises about a possible air disaster in terms not dissimilar to the opening passages of *The Satanic Verses*.

20 *TSV*, p. 439.

21 Peter van den Veer, 'Satanic or Angelic? The Politics of Religious and Literary Inspiration', in *Public Culture*, Fall 1989, pp. 100–104.

22 Brennan, *op. cit.*, p. 152.

23 Quoted in Gayatri Chakravorty Spivak, 'Reading the Satanic Verses', in *Public Culture, loc. cit.*, p. 87.

24 *TSV*, p. 319.

25 Spivak, *op. cit.*, p. 84.

26 *TSV*, p. 318.

27 van den Veer, *op. cit.*, p. 103.

28 Spivak, *op. cit.*, p. 83.

29 *TSV*, p. 209

30 *ibid.*, p. 79.

31 Brennan, *op. cit.*, p. 164.

32 Jussawalla, *op. cit.*, p. 114.

33 *New Yorker*, 15.5.89, p. 127.

34 *New York Times Magazine*, 24.1.89.

35 *Sunday Times Magazine,* 11.9.88.
36 *TSV,* p. 180.
37 *Desert Island Discs, op. cit.*
38 *Independent Magazine,* 10.9.88.
39 *TSV,* p. 17.
40 *ibid.,* p. 312.
41 *Independent Magazine, loc. cit.*
42 *TSV,* p. 30.
43 Lawson, *op. cit.*
44 *TSV,* p. 30.
45 *ibid.,* p. 97.
46 *ibid.,* p. 381.
47 *ibid.,* p. 386.
48 See Maxime Rodinson, *Mohammed,* tr. Anne Carter (Harmondsworth, 1971), pp. 207 ff.
49 *TSV,* p. 380.
50 *ibid.,* p. 392.
51 Denis MacEoin: unpublished paper kindly made available to author.
52 *TSV,* p. 427.
53 van den Veer, *op. cit.,* p. 100.

Chapter 2: Honour and Shame

1 *Guardian,* 27.2.89.
2 *The Rushdie File, op. cit.,* p. 224.
3 *ibid.,* p. 209.
4 Qur'an, 4:34.
5 Michael Gilsenan, *Recognising Islam: An Anthropologist's Introduction* (London, 1982), p. 117.
6 See Maxime Rodinson, *Mohammed, op. cit.;* W. Montgomery Watt, *Muhammad at Mecca* (Oxford, 1952); *Muhammad at Medina* (Oxford, 1956); Michael Cook, *Muhammad* (Oxford, 1983).
7 Qur'an, 7:188; *cf.* also 6:50 and 41:5.
8 A. Guillaume, *The Life of Muhammad: A Translation of Ishaq's Sirat Rasul Allah* (Oxford, 1987), p. 69.
9 *ibid.,* p. 72.
10 Annemarie Schimmel, *And Muhammad His Messenger: The Veneration of the Prophet in Islamic Piety* (North Carolina, 1985), p. 152.

11 *ibid.*, p. 35.

12 *ibid.*, p. 43.

13 *ibid.*, pp. 39, 79, 80.

14 *ibid.*, p. 42.

15 *ibid*, pp. 69–71.

16 Qur'an, 24:35.

17 Schimmel, *op. cit.*, p.125.

18 *ibid.*, p. 125.

19 *ibid.*, p. 130.

20 *ibid.*, p. 131.

21 *ibid.*, p. 138.

22 *ibid.*, p. 138.

23 *Oxford English Dictionary*, sv 'Mahound'.

24 H. Prideaux, *The True Nature &c* (London, 1718); an article on Rev. George Bush's *The Life of Mohammed* (New York, 1831) appeared in *Newsday*, New York, 28.2.89. I am grateful to Dr Goldman for supplying a copy.

25 Quoted in Normal Daniel, *Islam and the West: The Making of an Image* (Edinburgh, 1960), p. 27.

26 *ibid.*, pp. 99, 100.

27 *ibid.*, p. 104.

28 *TSV*, p. 93.

29 Feroza Jussawalla, 'Resurrecting the Prophet: The Case of Salman the Otherwise' in *Public Culture, loc. cit.*, p. 104.

30 Qur'an, 53:19–20. Tabari's version of the story of the Satanic Verses may be found in Guillaume, *op. cit.*, pp. 165 ff.

31 Qur'an, 53:21.

32 See Muhammad Asad, *The Message of the Qur'an* (Gibraltar, 1980), p. 814 n. 14.

33 Schimmel, *op. cit.*, pp. 29–31.

34 T. B. Irvine in *Impact International*, London, 23.6.89.

35 The Holy Qur'an, with English Translation and Commentary by Malik Ghulam Farid, p. 726 n.

36 See Helmut Gatje, *The Qur'an and its Exegesis*, tr. Alford Welch (Berkeley, 1976), p. 52.

37 Abu Abdallah bin Ahmad al Ansari al Quturbi, *Al jami li ahkam il qur'an*, Vol. 21, p. 80.

38 Baidawi, *Anwar al tanzil* (Constantinople, 1328H), p. 447.

39   Muhieddin al Darwish, *'Irat al qur'an al karim wa bayyanuhu* (Homs, 1983), Vol. 6, p. 450ff.

40   John Burton, 'Those are the High-Flying Cranes', *Journal of Semitic Studies*, Vol. XV (January 1970), p. 246ff.

41   Annemarie Schimmel, *Mystical Dimensions of Islam* (Chapel Hill, 1975), p. 28.

42   Yacoub Zaki, *The Times*, 28.2.89.

43   Marshall G. S. Hodgson, *The Venture of Islam* (Chicago, 1975), Vol. 1, p. 300.

44   *TSV*, p. 94.

45   *ibid.*, p. 95.

46   *ibid.*, p. 98.

47   *ibid.*

48   Qur'an, 2:118, 219–20; 39; 49–51.

49   *ibid.*, 26; 225.

50   Ibn Hisham, cited in Rodinson, *op. cit.*, pp. 157–8.

51   *ibid.*, p. 171.

52   R. A. Nicholson, *A Literary History of the Arabs* (Cambridge, 1930), p. 166.

53   *ibid.*, p. 318.

54   *ibid.*, p. 323.

55   Brennan, *op. cit.*, p. 143.

56   *TSV*, p. 364.

57   Abdulwahab Bouhdiba, *Sexuality in Islam*, tr. Alan Sheridan (London, 1985), p. 50.

58   Akbar S. Ahmed, 'Death in Islam: The Hawkes Bay Case', in *Man: Journal of the Royal Anthropological Institute*, Vol. 21, 1986, pp. 121–34. I am grateful to Bruce Lawrence for drawing my attention to the incident and to this article.

59   Spivak, *loc. cit.*, p. 82.

60   Schimmel, *And Muhammad . . .*, *op. cit.*, p. 32.

61   Hans Kung, *On Being A Christian*, tr. E. Quinn (London, 1977), p. 287.

62   See Malise Ruthven, *Torture: The Grand Conspiracy* (London, 1978), pp. 32–3 and *passim*.

63   Nicholas Walter, *Blasphemy in Britain* (London, 1977), *passim*.

64   *ibid.*

65   Joseph L. Conn; 'Blasphemy Laws in America: "A Great Embarrassment'", in *Church & State*, April 1989, p. 981.

66   ibid., loc. cit.

67   *Kitab al sarim al maslul ala shatim al rasul* (Hyderabad, 1905); see also Thomas Michel in Ibn Taymiyya, *A Muslim Theologian's Response to Christianity*, pp. 69–71.

68   Ibn Taymiyya, *Le traité de droit publique d'Ibn Taymiyya*, tr. H. Laoust (Beirut, 1948), p. 172.

69   Majid Khadduri, *War and Peace in the Law of Islam* (Baltimore, 1955), p. 26.

70   ibid., p. 97.

Chapter 3: Islam in Britain

1   Aziz Ahmed, *Studies in Islamic Culture in the Indian Environment* (Oxford, 1964), pp. 73–4.

2   A. L. Basham, *The Indian Subcontinent in Historical Perspective* (London, 1958); quoted in Ahmed, *op. cit.*, p. 75.

3   Rudolph Peters, *Islam and Colonialism: The Doctrine of Jihad in Modern History* (The Hague, 1979), p. 46.

4   ibid., p. 52.

5   B. D. Metcalf, *Islamic Revival in British India: Deoband 1860–1900* (Princeton, 1982), pp. 296 ff.; Francis Robinson, *Varieties of South Asian Islam* (Coventry Centre for Research in Ethnic Relations, 1988), p. 9.

6   See B. D. Metcalf, 'Islamic Reform and Islamic Women' and Maulana Thanawi, 'Jewelry of Paradise' in B. D. Metcalf (ed.), *Moral Conduct and Authority* (Berkeley, 1984), pp. 184–95.

7   Robinson, *op. cit.*, pp. 15–16; Felice Dassetto, 'The Tabligh Organisation in Belgium' in Tomas Gerholm and Yngve Georg Lithman (eds.), *The New Islamic Presence in Western Europe* (London, 1988), pp. 159–74.

8   W. Cantwell Smith, 'Ahmadiyya' in *Encyclopaedia of Islam* (Leiden, 1960), 2nd edn.; Robinson, *op. cit.*, pp. 13–14.

9   Sayyid Abu'l Ala Maududi, *The Religion of Truth* (Lahore, 1967), pp. 3–4.

10   ibid., loc. cit.

11   ibid., p. 390.

12   Sayyid Abu'l Ala Maududi, *Purdah and the Status of Women in Islam* (Lahore, 1979) and *Birth Control* (Lahore, 1978); cf. Malise Ruthven, *Islam in the World* (Harmondsworth and New York, 1984), p. 328.

13   Dervla Murphy, *Tales from Two Cities: Travels of Another Sort* (London 1988), p. 110.

14   Badr Dahya, 'Pakistani Ethnicity in Industrial Cities in Britain', in Abner Cohen (ed.), *Urban Ethnicity* (London, 1974), p. 80.

15   Murphy, *op. cit.*, p. 111.

16   Murphy, *ibid.*, p. 53.

17   Cohen, *op. cit.*, p. 112.

18   Daniele Joly, 'Making a Place for Islam in British Society: Muslims in Birmingham', in Gerholm and Lithman, *op. cit.*, p. 32.

19   Amrit Wilson, *Finding a Voice: Asian Women in Britain* (London, 1978), p. 5.

20   Gilsenan, *op. cit.*, p. 118.

21   Wilson, *op. cit.*, p. 31.

22   Murphy, *op. cit.*, p. 19.

23   *ibid.*, pp. 25, 52.

24   *ibid.*, p. 22.

25   *ibid.*, pp. 111–12.

26   *ibid.*, p. 124.

27   *ibid.*, p. 137.

28   *ibid.*, p. 28.

29   Jorgen S. Nielsen, 'Muslims in Britain and Local Authority Responses' in Gerholm and Lithman, *op. cit.*, p. 75.

30   *Education for All: The Report of the Committee of Inquiry into the Education of Children from Ethnic Minority Groups*, Cmnd. 9453 (London, HMSO, 1986), p. 518.

31   Quoted in Edward Hulmes, *Education and Cultural Diversity* (London, 1989), pp. 43–4.

32   *ibid.*, p. 44.

Chapter 4:   Conspiracy

1   *Sunday*, 2.10.89, p. 78.

2   *Illustrated Weekly of India*, 12.3.89.

3   *The Times of India*, 13.10.89; quoted in *The Rushdie File, op. cit.*, p. 47.

4   *India Today*, 15.9.88; quoted in *The Rushdie File, op. cit.*, p. 401.

5 *Sunday*, 18–24.9.88; quoted in *The Rushdie File*, *op. cit.*, p. 41.

6 *ibid.*, p. 48.

7 N. Gerald Barrier, *BANNED: Controversial Literature and Political Control in British India, 1907–1947* (St Louis, 1974). See also Schimmel, *And Muhammad*, *op. cit.*, p. 66.

8 Kindly supplied to me by Dinpankar Sarkar.

9 *The Rushdie File*, *op. cit.*, p. 44.

10 *Illustrated Weekly of India*, 7.10.89, p. 12.

11 *Impact International*, London, 14–27.10.88, p. 15.

12 *Illustrated Weekly of India*, 12.3.89, p. 15.

13 *The Rushdie File*, *op. cit.*, p. 64.

14 Shabbir Akhtar, *Be Careful with Muhammad* (London, 1989), p. 17, 28–9.

15 Kalim Siddiqui (ed.), *Issues in the Islamic Movement, 1982–3* (London, 1984), pp. 15–16.

16 Steve Bruce, *The Rise and Fall of the New Christian Right: Conservative Protestant Politics in America, 1978–1988* (Oxford, 1988), p. 79.

17 In Siddiqui, *op. cit.*, pp. 362–3.

Chapter 5:   Ayatollahs of the North

1 *Impact International*, 10–23.2.89, p. 10.

2 Quoted in the *Guardian*, 15.2.89.

3 *Independent*, 21.2.89.

4 *ibid.*

5 David Hirst, *Weekend Guardian*, 4–5.2.89, p. 41.

6 *Independent*, 22.2.89.

7 *Observer*, 19.2.89.

8 BBC *Summary of World Broadcasts*, 20.2.89.

9 *Daily Telegraph*, 23.2.89.

10 *Illustrated Weekly of India*, 12.3.89.

11 *Independent*, 17.3.89.

12 *The Times*, 15.2.89.

13 *Daily Express*, 20.2.89.

14 *Guardian*, 16.2.89.

15 *Star*, 21.2.89.

16 *Today*, 16.2.89.

17 *The Rushdie File*, *op. cit.*, p. 240.

18 *Crescent International*, Toronto, 1–5.2.89, p. 7.

19 *Observer*, 2.4.89; see also *Rushdie File, op. cit.*, p. 251.

20 cf. Murphy, *op. cit.*, p. 14.

Chapter 6:   The Word and the Text

1 Werner Schiffauer, 'Migration and Religiousness', in Gerholm and Lithman, *op. cit.*, pp. 147, 149.

2 *ibid.*, pp. 150–1.

3 *ibid.*, p. 155.

4 Qur'an, 2:23.

5 Gilkes Keppel, Lecture delivered at Dartmouth College, New Hampshire, November 1989.

6 Majid Fakhry, *A History of Islamic Philosophy* (London, 1988), pp. 178–9.

7 Frithjof Schuon, *Understanding Islam*, tr. D. M. Matheson (London, 1976), p. 44.

8 Michael Cook, *Muhammed* (Oxford, 1983), p. 67.

9 *ibid.*, p. 74.

10 *ibid.*, p. 69.

11 John Wansburgh, *Qur'anic Studies* (Oxford, 1977), p. 47.

12 Malise Ruthven, *The Divine Supermarket* (London, 1989), pp. 173 ff.

13 Walter J. Ong, *Orality and Literacy* (London, 1982), p. 34.

14 Thomas Carlyle, *On Heroes and Hero Worship* (originally published as *Heroes, Hero-worship and the Heroic in History*, 1841); edn. with *Sartor Resartus* (London, 1914), p. 299.

15 cf. Ong, *op. cit.*, p. 147.

16 *ibid.*, p. 901.

17 *ibid.*, p. 119.

18 *ibid.*, p. 12.

19 *ibid.*, p. 101.

20 *ibid.*, p. 72.

21 *ibid.*, p. 69.

22 *ibid.*, p. 74.

23 *ibid.*, p. 68.

24 *ibid.*, p. 33.

25 *ibid.*, p. 159.

26 *ibid.*, p. 154.

Conclusion

1 *Crescent International*, Vol. 18, No. 17, 1–15.11.89.
2 *The Independent*, 16.12.89.
3 *ibid.*, 28.10.89.
4 Charles Taylor, in *Public Culture*, *op cit.*, p. 120.
5 *ibid.*, p. 121.
6 *ibid.*
7 *New Statesman and Society*, 15.12.89.
8 *PN Review*, Vol. 15, No. 4, pp. 15–16.
9 Wole Soyinka 'Jihad for Freedom', *Index on Censorship* 18.5, May/June 1989, p. 20.
10 *Observer*, 1.10.89.
11 Gayatri Chakravorty Spivak, 'Reading The Satanic Verses' in *Public Culture*, Vol. 2, No. 1, Fall 1989, p. 87.
12 Feroza Jussawalla, 'Resurrecting the Prophet: the Case of Salman the Otherwise' in *Public Culture*, Vol. 2, No. 1, Fall 1989, p. 107.

Acknowledgements

This book could never have been completed in the short time available without the research assistance of Elfi Pallis and Russell Harris. My thanks to Elfi for directing my attention to key articles in the British and foreign press; and to Russell for his scholarly help in digging up English and Arabic texts. Lisa Appignanesi supplied further documentation, as did Kevin Boyle and John Hoyland of Article 19 and The Friends of Salman Rushdie; Josephine Pullein-Thompson and Tom Aitken of PEN (UK) were also helpful with documents, as were Elizabeth Patterson of International PEN, Gara LaMarche of PEN (USA), New York, and Carol Keyes of People for the American Way in Washington, DC. I am indebted to Amy Arlin for help with computer discs and to Melissa Zeiger for use of her printer and word-processor. Grey and Neiti Gowrie generously provided space – and a peaceful environment – to work in. Others who helped directly or indirectly in the preparation of this book include: Raficq Abdullah, Jallal Ahmed, Tanwir Ahmed, Gillon Aitken, Shabbir Akhtar, Sher Azam, Zaki Badawi, Louis Baum, Karen Brown, Liz Calder, Carmen Callil, David Caute, Michael Cook, Isabel Fonseca, Gene Garthwaite, Fred Halliday, Ishtiaq Hamed, Paul Harper, Anne Huggins, Edward Hulmes, George Joffé, Sukie Karey, Paul Keegan, Jaafar Karim, Tony Lacey, Philip Lewis, Denis MacEoin, Kenan Malik, Baqir Moin, Kumar Murshed, Mushtaq Parker, Adrian Pennink, Barney Platts-Mills, Paul Richard, Deborah Rogers, Marianne Rohlen, Dipankar Sarkar, Nicholas Shakespeare, Muhammad Siddiqi, Andrew Wylie.

The idea for doing this book first arose when Isabel Quigley and John Wilkins of the *Tablet* sent me *The Satanic Verses* for review. I wish to thank Tiggy Ruthven for her invaluable suggestions at the editorial stage, and Jeremy Lewis of Chatto and Windus for editorial help and for his patience.

With a subject that arouses such deep passions as the Rushdie Affair, it takes more than the conventional disclaimer to exonerate those mentioned from any responsibility for errors or opinions in the text. I must emphasise that while I learned much from conversations and interviews with all those mentioned, the opinions and conclusions in this book are entirely my own: I take full responsibility for everything printed.

The author and publishers are grateful to the publishers of the following works for permission to quote from them: to Penguin Books for *The Satanic Verses* by Salman Rushdie; to Jonathan Cape for *Shame* by Salman Rushdie; to Routledge/Croom Helm for Michael Gilsenan's *Recognising Islam*; to the University of North Carolina Press for *And Muhammad His Messenger* by Annemarie Schimmel; to E. J. Brill for *Islam and Colonialism* by Rudolph Peters; to John Murray and Penguin Books for *Tales from Two Cities: Travels of Another Sort* by Dervla Murphy; to Mansell Publishing for *The New Islamic Presence in Western Europe* edited by Tomas Gerholm and Yngve Georg Lithman; and to Methuen for *Orality and Literacy* by Walter Ong.

London December 1989

Index

Abdullah ibn Sa'ad, 39
Abel, Armand, 47
Abu Hureira, 38
Abu'l Ala la Ma'ari, 43
Abu Sufyan, 41
Adams, John, 50
Ahl-i-Hadith ('Hadith Folk'), 33, 40,
    61–2
Ahmad, Khurshid, 66
Ahmad, Mirza Ghulam, 63
Ahmadiyya, the, 62–3
Ahmed, Faiyazuddin, 92
Ahsan, Dr M. M., 91–2, 95, 97
Ajeeb, Mohammad, 77
Akbar, Mughal Emperor, 57
Akhtar, Dr Shabbir, 96, 120, 121–30,
    142, 161
Al Azhar, Cairo, 54
Al Baidawi, 39
al Ghamdi, Dr Mughram, 95, 96,
    105
al Ghazali: *Ihya ulum al din*, 34
al Husseini, Hajj Amin, 104
Ali, 2, 46, 47
al-Jili, Abdul Karim, 33
Allende, Isabel, 13
al Mamun, Caliph, 40
Al Quturbi, 39
al Tustari, Sahl, 32–3

Anwar, 96, 131, 132–42
Arnald of Cîteaux, 48
Asad, Muhammad (Leopold
    Weiss), 6, 30, 135–6
Ashdown, Paddy, MP, 118
Asma bint Marwan, 42
Augustine, St, 128, 129
Ayesha, 44–5, 46–7
Ayodhya, shrine of (Uttar Pradesh),
    85–6
Azam, Sher, 76, 81–5, 90, 91, 97–8,
    98–9, 105, 117
Aziz, Shah Abdul, 57
Azzam, Dr Salem, 95

Bachan, Amitabh, 16
Badawi, Dr Zaki, 29, 47
Baker, Kenneth, MP, 105
Banerji, Chitrita, 85
Banu Qurayza, the, 48
Barelwi, Ahmad Riza Khan, 60, 67
Barelwi, Sayyid Ahmed, 57–8
Barelwis, the, 60, 66, 67
Basti, Akhundazeh, 113
Basu, Shrabani, 15, 86
Baz, Sheikh Bin, 136
Bell, Steve, 14
Bhutto, Benazir, 66, 107–8
Bhutto, Zulfikar Ali, 12, 13, 63

blasphemy laws,
   in Britain, 48–50, 52, 155, 156–7
   Indian (Article 295A), 86–8
   Islamic, 51–2, 122, 126, 127
   in USA, 50–1, 52–3, 122, 155
Bloomsbury Publishing Ltd, 22–3
Bolton, Muslim demonstration in,
   104
Bombay, demonstration against
   British Council in, 114
Booker Prize, the, 22
Borges, Jorge Luis, 44, 132
Boyle, Kevin, 99
Bradford, 68
   Bradford and Ickley Community
      College conference (1989), 131–3
   burning of *Satanic Verses* in, 81,
      97, 103
   Council of Mosques, 76, 81–2, 90,
      95, 104–5, 120, 122
   Indo-Pakistani settlers in, 68–72
   Ray Honeyford affair, 75–8
Brennan, Timothy, 13–14, 19, 43
Britain, Muslim communities in,
   54–5, 66–72, 157
   effect of *fatwa* on, 118–19, 120–1,
   152
Bruce, Steve, 100–1
Bukhari, Imam, 85, 114–15
Burton, John, 39
Bush, Rev. George: *Life of
   Mohammed*, 35

Caetani, Count, 39
Calder, Liz, 22
Cambridge University, 21
Campbellpuris, the, 68, 69, 70
Central Mosque, Regent's Park,
   London, 54, 95, 96, 105, 157
Chowdery, Moinuddin, 67–8
Christianity,
   and blasphemy, 47, 48–9, 155

comparisons with Islam, 6, 29, 30,
   135, 136
a Muslim view of, 3
the spread of, 146–7
Clark, Justice Tom, 50
Cook, Michael, 31, 144, 145
Cooper, Roger, 110
Council of Mosques, Bradford, 76,
   81–2, 90, 95, 104–5, 120, 122
Crescent International, 123

Daily Express, 119
Dante Alighieri: *Inferno*, 2–3
Dar al Harb, 51, 52, 119
Dar al Islam, 51, 52, 119
Davidson, Robyn, 23–4
Day of Muslim Solidarity, 152
Dayha, Badr, 71
Death of a Princess, 92
Deccan Herald, 88
Deobandis, the, 60–1, 66, 85
'Desert Island Discs', 11, 12
Dickie, Dr James, 101
Dicks, Terry, MP, 119
Drummond Middle School,
   Bradford, 75–8
Dumas, Roland, 110

Eco, Umberto, 160
Eddy, Mary Baker, 15
education, religious, 79–80
Ejaz, Ahmed, 92
el Azhar, Sheikh, 54
el Essawy, Hesham, 96–7, 105

Fahad, King, of Saudi Arabia, 66, 92
Farid, Malik Ghulam, 39
Faruqi, M. H., 93–5, 105
fatiha, 4
Fatima, 46, 47
Fatima, Naseem, 45–7
fatwa, Khomeini's, 11, 112, 113

and after-effects, 114–18
British government's reaction to, 118
British Muslims' reaction to, 118–20, 151–2
Saudi Arabian reaction to, 117
Feisal, King, 136
Fifth of June Foundation, 113
fiqh, 44
Fox, Marcus, MP, 76
fundamentalism, Islamic, 129, 135, 136, 142

Gandhi, Indira, 12, 16
Gandhi, Mahatma, 60
Gandhi, Rajiv, 85, 88, 89, 90, 159
Gandhi, Sanjay, 12
Gay News, 49
Genet, Jean: *Le Balcon*, 26
Gerald of Wales, 36
Gilani, Abdul Qadir, 60
Gilsenan, Michael, 30, 73
Gish, Duane, 19
Goldziher, Ignaz, 38
Guardian, the, 29, 122
Guardian of Islam, 111
Gulf War, the, 107, 110

hadith-collectors, 38, 139–40
'Hadith Folk', *see* Ahl-i-Hadith
Hailey, William, 87
halal killings, 44, 75
Hamilton, Judge King, 49
Haqq, General Zia ul, *see* Zia ul Haqq
Hawkes Bay, Karachi, 45–6, 96
Hindus and Hinduism, 55–7, 85–6, 88, 102
Hitler, Adolf, 103, 104
Honeyford, Ray, 75–8, 104
Howe, Sir Geoffrey, 110, 118
Hoyland, John, 99

Hubbard, L. Ron, 15, 127
Hulmes, Professor Edward, 80
Hussein, Imam, 46
Hussein, Ishtiaq, 96
Hussein, Liaqat, 90, 99–100, 102–3
Hussein, Saddam, 107

Ibn Battuta, 19
Ibn Hanbal, Ahmad, 40, 67
Ibn Kathir, 39
Ibn Sa'd, 37
Ibn Taymiyya, 51, 153
Ibn Thabit, Hassan, 42
Ibn ul Arabi, 33
Ignatieff, Michael, 126
ijtihad, 40
Illustrated Weekly of India, The, 89–90, 92
Ilyas, Maulana Muhammad, 62
Imam, the Hidden, 4
imams, 72
Immigration Act (1962), 70
Impact International, 91, 92, 93, 105, 106
Independent, the, 151
India,
   blasphemy laws in (Article 295A), 86–8
   Islam in, 55–63
   Satanic Verses proscribed in, 85, 88–90
Indian Express, 88
Indian Mutiny (1857), 58
India Today, 14, 86
Iqbal, Muhammad, 43
Iran,
   early reactions to *Satanic Verses*, 108–10
   liberalisation within, 111
   war with Iraq, 107, 110
   see also Khomeini, Ayatollah

Islam,
  as system of law, 154
  assumption of dominance, 154–5
  essentialist viewpoint, 158
  faith and sexuality in, 29–31
  fundamentalist, 129, 135, 136, 142
  in India, 55–63
  nominalist viewpoint, 158, 159
  orality of, 145–9
  view of women, 6, 7–8, 73–5, 129,
    130
  see also Qur'an, the
Islamabad, storming of US
    embassy, 108
Islamic Conference Organisation,
    92, 117, 120–1
Islamic Cultural Centre, London,
    54–5, 66
Islamic Defence Council, 105–6
Islamic Democratic Alliance (IDA),
    107
Islamic Foundation, Leicester, 91,
    92
Islamic Foundation, Madras, 92
Islamic Mission, UK, 66, 95
isnad, 38
izzat, 7–8, 36, 73–5, 162

jahiliya, 41
Jain, Madhu, 14, 86
Jamaat-i-Islami (Maududists), 15,
    63–8, 82, 92, 107–8, 137, 138,
    152–3
Jamaat Tabligh ul Islam, 62, 99, 121
Jefferson, Thomas, 50
Jews,
  Muslim views on, 3
  suspected of anti-Islamic
    conspiracy, 99–100, 101
  see also Zionists
jihad (Holy War), 48, 52, 58–9
Johnson, R. W., 157

Joseph, Sir Keith, MP, 76
Jussawalla, Feroza, 19, 36, 161

Kaufman, Gerald, MP, 151
Kayhan Farangi, 108–9
Kemal Ataturk, 54
Khamenei, President Ali, 113, 115
Khan, Kurshid Alam, 89
Khan, Sayyid Ahmed, 58–9, 65
khilafa, 7
Khomeini, Ahmed, 110, 112
Khomeini, Ayatollah, 5, 11, 15, 64,
    107, 109, 110, 111–17, 136, 152,
    153
Kirkup, James: 'The Love That Dare
    To Speak Its Name', 49

Law Commission, the, 49–50
Lawson, Mark, 22
Leithauser, Brad, 15, 20
Lemon, Denis, 49
Llosa, Mario Vargas, 13
Luard, Clarissa, 21
Lytton, Lord, 59

MacEoin, Denis, 27
Madden, Max, MP, 4
Mahfouz, Neguib, 116, 123, 153
Mahound, 35–6
Mailer, Norman, 99
Malik ibn Anas, 52
Manchester, Muslim disputes in, 67
Marquez, Gabriel Garcia, 13, 45, 132
Marzorati, Gerald, 20, 23
Mason, Roger Burford, 159
Maududi, Maulana Abu'l Ala, 63–5,
    66
Maududist Islamic Foundation, 95
Maududists, *see* Jamaat-i-Islami
Mayer, Peter, 85
Mazrui, Dr Ali, 29, 47
Meer, Abdul Kadir, 90–1

Merchant, Ismail, 19
Mirpuris, the, 68, 69, 70, 77–8
Montefiore, Bishop Hugh: *Myth of God Incarnate*, 49
Mormons, the, 26, 53, 140
mosques, British Muslim, 71–2; in Bradford, 81–2
  see also Central Mosque, Regent's Park
Mourou, Abdel Fatah, 116
Moussavi, Hussein, 110
Mu'tazilis, the, 40
Mughal emperors, 55, 57
Muhammad, Prophet, 5, 6, 15, 31–5, 161–2
  Dante's treatment of, 2–3
  in the Qur'an, 31, 141, 144, 145, 147
  Satanic Verses as attack on, 7, 8–9, 28, 30–1, 35–40, 43–4, 47–8, 90, 91–2
Muhammadan Literary Society of Calcutta, 58
Muir, Sir William, 39
Mukherjee, Bharati, 13
multiculturalism, 78–80
Murphy, Dervla, 69, 74, 75, 77, 78
musafihat, 7
Muslim Brotherhood, 63
Muslim Institute, the, 100
Muslim Integration Council, 114
Muslims, *see under* Britain; Islam
muttakidhat akhdan, 7

Nadiri, Manlan Hasan Ali, 115
Nai Duniya, 90
Namboodiri, P. K. N.: 'Mohammad the Idiot', 88
Naqshbandi order, 57
Nasr i Khusraw, 43
Nasser, Gamal Abdul, 63

Ogilvy and Mather, 21
Ong, Walter, 147, 148
orality, Islamic, 145–9
Ortega, Daniel, 13
Oval Theatre, Kennington, 21

Pakistan,
  anti-Ahmadiyya agitation in, 63
  demonstrations against *Satanic Verses* in, 107–8
  Deobandi opposition to, 61
  Jamaat-i-Islami in, 63, 65–6
Pakistani settlers in Britain, 68–71
Pakistan's People's Party (PPP), 107
Pathans, the, 60, 73
patriarchy, Islamic, 6, 7
Patten, John, MP, 151
Penguin Books India, 85
Penguin/Viking, UK, 94, 96, 97, 98, 102–3, 105, 152, 159, 160
Perdition, 128
Prideaux, Humphrey: *The True Nature of the Imposture Fully Displayed by the Life of Mahomet*, 35
Prophet, the, *see* Muhammad, the Prophet
Protocols of the Elders of Zion, The, 101

Quddus, Sayyid Abdul, 103, 104, 119–20
Qur'an, the, 3, 55, 136–7, 140–1, 142, 143–7
  Asad's English translation of, 6, 30, 135–6
  Barelwi's Urdu translation of, 67
  faith and sexuality in, 30–1
  God as revealed in, 5
  male supremacy in, 6, 7
  Muhammad portrayed in, 31, 141, 144, 145, 147
  Satanic Verses as attack on, 7, 8–9, 40–4, 138–9

Qutb, Sayyid, 63

racism, 78, 126–7, 156, 157
Rafsanjani, Ali Hashemi, 110, 112,
   115
Rahman, Fazlur, 39
Rahman, Sheikh Umar Abdul, 116,
   123, 153
Rajneesh, Baghwan Shree, 115
Rajpal (Lahore bookseller), 87
Rangila Rasul (The Merry Prophet), 87
Rao, N. T. Rama, 16
Rao, V. N. Subba, 88
Razi, 39
Renaissance Movement, Tunisia,
   116
Richardson, Samuel, 21
Rodinson, Maxime, 31, 39
Roth, Philip, 99
Rugby School, 20
Rushdie, Anis Ahmed, 21
Rushdie, Marianne *see* Wiggins,
   Marianne
Rushdie, Salman, 10, 158–63
   autobiographical details in *Satanic*
      Verses, 20–4
   on 'Desert Island Discs', 11, 12
   Grimus, 22
   Illustrated Weekly of India article,
      89–90
   interviews in Indian magazines,
      15, 86
   issues apology, 113–14
   The Jaguar Smile, 158
   Khomeini's *fatwa* pronounced on,
      112, 113
   Midnight's Childen, 12, 13, 14, 16,
      22, 108, 158
   'open letter' to Rajiv Gandhi, 89,
      159
   perception of political truth, 12,
      13

Satanic Verses *see separate entry*
Shame, 12, 13, 14, 17, 22, 65–6,
   108, 158, 159

Said, Edward, 38
salaat, 71
Saladin, 16
Salisbury Review, 75
Salman al Farisi, 39
Sanei, Hojjat-ul-Islam Sheikh, 113
Sarkar, Jadunath, 56
Satanic Verses, The, 2, 11, 127,
   159–61, 163
   as attack on Muhammad and the
      Qur'an, 7, 8–9, 28, 30–1, 35–44,
      47–8, 90, 91–2, 138–9
   autobiographical elements in,
      20–4
   Sher Azam's views on, 84–5,
      91–2, 98–9
   banning of in Muslim countries,
      94, 95
   Bradford conference on, 131–3
   brothel scene in, 25–7, 28
   burning of, 81, 97, 103
   Indian government ban on, 85,
      88–90
   Iranian reactions to, 108–14
   mixing of fact and fiction in, 44,
      46, 47
   origin of title, 37–9
   plot and sub-plots in, 16–20,
      24–5, 27
   Rushdie on, 14, 15, 113
Sau'd, King Abdul Aziz ibn, 135
Saud, Prince, 117
Saudi Arabia, 62, 92, 107
   funding from, 66–7
   reaction to *fatwa*, 117
Sayyids, 45, 46
Schiffauer, Werner, 134, 135
Schimmel, Annemarie, 32

Schuon, Frithjof, 144
Scorsese, Martin: *The Last Temptation*, 47
Scruton, Roger, 75
Seit, Suleiman, 89
Shaban, Sheikh, 115
Shaddad ibn al Aswad al Laythi, 42–3
Shahabuddin, Syed, MP, 85–6, 89, 115
Shari'a courts, 153, 154
Shi'a, the, 4, 39, 45, 46, 47, 113, 122
shirk, 33, 142
Siddiq, Muhammad, 121
Siddiqui, Dr Kalim, 100, 151–2, 153, 160
Sidiqi, Shahid, 90
Sikhs, the, 58
Singh, Justice Dalap, 87
Singh, Khushwant, 85
Sirhindi, Sheikh Ahmed, 57
Smith, Joseph, 15, 26, 53
Soghal, Gita, 18
Sontag, Susan, 99
South Africa, banning of *Satanic Verses* in, 95
Southall Black Sisters, 18
Southern Journal of Philosophy, 123
Soyinka, Wole, 159
Spivak, Gayatri, 18, 47, 161
Sufism, 39, 57, 59
Sun, the, 119–20, 151
Sunday, 15, 85, 86
Sunnis, the, 4, 6, 33–4, 40, 46, 47, 54, 62, 142–3
Sunni Tawhid movement, Lebanon, 115
Supreme Guardianship Council, 109
Swann Committee, the, 79–80
Sylhetis, the, 69, 70

Tabari, 37, 39
Tablighi Jamaat, *see* Jamaat Tabligh ul Islam
talaq, 7
Tantawi, Sheikh, 115–16
taqiya, 122
Tariqa-i-Muhammadi (Path of Muhammad), 58
Taylor, Charles, 156
Telegraph and Argus, 103
Thatcher, Margaret, 76, 91, 118
Thousand and One Nights, The, 11, 17
Times, The, 103, 104
Times of India, The, 86
Today, 120
Turkey,
  ban on *Satanic Verses*, 154
  Muslim peasants, 134–5

'ubudiyya, 7
ulema, 61, 64, 65
Ullah, Baha, 15
Ullah, Shah Wali, 57
Umayr ibn Adi, 42
Umeed, 90
umma, 54, 56
Union of Mosques Organisation, 157
Union of Muslim Organisations, 95
  Guidelines . . . on Islamic Education, 80
United States,
  blasphemy laws in, 50–1, 52–3, 122, 155
  sales of *Satanic Verses* in, 161
'Uthman, Caliph, 144

Van den Veer, Peter, 28
Vaz, Keith, MP, 4
Velyati, Ali Akbar, 110

Wahhab, Muhammad ibn Abdul, 67

Walcott, Derek, 13
Wansburgh, John, 145
Warner, Marina, 29
Watt, W. Montgomery, 31, 39
Weiss, Leopold, *see* Asad,
    Muhammad
Wesley, John, 62
Whitechapel, London: Bengali
    mosque, 67
Whitehouse, Mary, 49
Wiggins, Marianne, 24, 113
William of Tyre, 35–6
Wilson, Amrit, 74
women, Islamic view of, 6, 7–8,
    73–5, 129, 130

Women Against Fundamentalism,
    5, 17–18
World Islamic League, 66
World Muslim League, 117
Wright, Ian, 132
Wright, Peter: *Spycatcher*, 101–2, 128

Yamani, Sheikh, 136
Yapp, Malcolm, 112
Yorkshire Post, 75, 76

Zaki, Yacoub, *see* Dickie, Dr James
Zamakhshari, 39
Zia ul Haqq, General, 12, 13, 65, 125
zina, 7, 8, 30
Zionists, 101, 104, 128